MW00806230

Epic Fails in American History

27 Historical Failures That Shaped Our Future and the Valuable Lessons Gained

© Copyright 2024- All rights reserved.

The content contained within this book may not be reproduced, duplicated, or transmitted without direct written permission from the author or the publisher.

Under no circumstances will any blame or legal responsibility be held against the publisher or author for any damages, reparation, or monetary loss due to the information contained within this book, either directly or indirectly.

Legal Notice:

This book is copyright-protected. It is only for personal use. You cannot amend, distribute, sell, use, quote, or paraphrase any part of the content within this book without the consent of the author or publisher.

Disclaimer Notice:

Please note the information contained within this document is for educational and entertainment purposes only. All effort has been executed to present accurate, up-to-date, reliable, and complete information. No warranties of any kind are declared or implied. Readers acknowledge that the author is not engaging in the rendering of legal, financial, medical, or professional advice. The content within this book has been derived from various sources. Please consult a licensed professional before attempting any techniques outlined in this book.

By reading this document, the reader agrees that under no circumstances is the author responsible for any losses, direct or indirect, that are incurred as a result of the use of the information contained within this document, including, but not limited to, errors, omissions, or inaccuracies.

Welcome Aboard, Check Out This Limited-Time Free Bonus!

Ahoy, reader! Welcome to the Ahoy Publications family, and thanks for snagging a copy of this book! Since you've chosen to join us on this journey, we'd like to offer you something special.

Check out the link below for a FREE e-book filled with delightful facts about American History.

But that's not all - you'll also have access to our exclusive email list with even more free e-books and insider knowledge. Well, what are ye waiting for? Click the link below to join and set sail toward exciting adventures in American History.

Access your bonus here

https://ahoypublications.com/

Or, Scan the QR code!

Table of Contents

Introduction

America's path from the early colonial era to independence and its eventual position as a superpower with global reach and influence was seldom smooth. In fact, it was a wild rollercoaster of violence, tensions, economic downturns, and all sorts of other human struggles that could only be overcome through the indomitable spirit that has come to define the American experience and progress. While turbulences of all kinds are certainly common features in the nascent state of most countries, the United States has followed a trajectory of historical development that has been and still is unique in many ways.

That trajectory has been determined by great successes, breakthroughs, and innovations by inventive minds worldwide, but it has also been shaped by significant blunders. These failures have profoundly affected the development of the United States as a country while also exerting tremendous influence on the mentality of the American people. Blunders of epic proportions have been common enough across the histories of most countries, but different nations have struggled with hardships that have revolved around their unique particularities. In America's case, some of these particularities have included racial and ethnic tensions in a highly diverse society, rapid capitalist development, and confrontational great power politics.

Nonetheless, the roots of failure and disaster tend to be rather universal, almost always involving some form of misjudgment, miscalculation, poor leadership, or other human follies that lead to consequences that are rarely intended. This book will delve into many such moments in American history, where fateful decisions and tragic circumstances have led to blunders, the ripple effects of which are felt to this day. The historic failures covered in this book will include those that have transpired in politics, economics, cultural life, warfare, and most other facets of American life. The book will chronicle these events through a comprehensive overview while also closely examining their causes and, just as importantly, the invaluable historical lessons they provide.

These pivotal missteps and their enduring impacts are as essential to study now as they've ever been. After all, nothing happens without history, as it is a continuous process that weaves its way through the centuries like an unbreakable thread connecting one event to the next. The more lessons drawn from past blunders, the easier it becomes for current and future generations to affect the events to come.

While this book might not resolve the burning issues of American politics in the present day, it will provide you with the knowledge necessary for meaningful historical reflection. Its objective is to be a comprehensive guide that's easy to understand, stimulates history enthusiasts, and is accessible to beginners. At the very least, it will teach or remind you that America's successes aren't to be taken for granted. The path that the American people have traversed to bring the United States to where it is today has been a long, thorny, and winding road, and the stories you are about to explore in the coming chapters will certainly bring that point home.

Chapter 1: Foundational Frictions

In the decades following the 1776 Declaration of Independence, the United States of America was a much smaller, different country experiencing all sorts of growing pains. Like any young state, the US had to consolidate itself economically and politically before it could stand firmly on its own legs in the aftermath of the British crown's departure. A notable feature of early American state-building, which still shows its residual effects, was a profound skepticism of federal authority.

Signing the declaration of independence.[1]

One of the key factors contributing to this emerging culture of opposition to centralization was the experience of tyranny under British rule in the Thirteen Colonies. Just ten years after the Thirteen Colonies became states and formed the independent union, problems associated with a weak central government began to emerge. As the Articles of Confederation prescribed a tightly constrained and underfunded government, expressing one's grievances through open revolt seemed like an appealing option in the absence of a strong federal military.

As such, the early decades of independent American history saw a number of revolts that produced significant crises. On the other hand, these troublesome years would ultimately demonstrate the incredible resilience and adaptability of the nascent post-colonial state. During this time, Americans demonstrated a well-developed capacity for deliberation, problem-solving, compromise, and state-building while ensuring the preservation of the liberties held so dearly by the American Revolution and its leaders.

Shays' Rebellion

The ever-contentious American issue of taxation was one of the key stumbling blocks hindering the young republic's attempts to consolidate and increase its cohesion. In the aftermath of the Revolutionary War, the United States had to contend with significant economic hardships, not least of which was the tens of millions of dollars in debts incurred to finance the war effort against Britain. At the time, these were substantial sums that weighed heavily on the undeveloped economy.

To make matters worse, the Thirteen Colonies had been naturally dependent on the empire regarding many aspects of their economies. Expectedly, the newly independent state's relationship with the British left a lot to be desired. British imports largely persisted out of necessity, but the British took action to limit American exports, barring the US from previously lucrative trade relations with parts of the British Empire.

Amid these difficulties, the federal government was left with very few choices on how to strengthen its finances. The most obvious option available was taxation, and as the new government gradually increased and expanded the taxes, it wasn't long until friction began to arise. In the 1780s, the economy in much of New England still revolved around subsistence farming, such as in western Massachusetts. It was largely a barter economy that relied on exchanging goods and services to settle trade between people. During the widespread economic downturn in the postwar years, many of the farmers in western, rural Massachusetts accumulated significant debts to the merchants and shopkeepers in the east. Normally, these obligations would have been settled with goods and services, but the merchants themselves encountered a new problem in the newly independent US.

Namely, the lines of credit they used to receive from their partners in Europe were discontinued, with these partners now demanding hard currency payments for their goods. To acquire this currency, the merchants began demanding payments from their American partners in the countryside, farmers who had little more than their produce to offer. The problem was a major shortage of hard currency across the US at this time, especially among the farmers in rural areas. In these conditions, the state decided to raise taxes to deal with its post-war debts and pay its obligations to the federal government. This led to a chain of demand for something generally scarce, with each layer of society and state pressing on those under them, causing tensions.

As 1786 came around, the Articles of Confederation had been in effect for a few years, severely restricting the federal government's powers. Keeping the government under tight constraints and balancing the power in America heavily in favor of the individual states was a popular idea as the memories of British tyranny were fresh. As popular as these anti-government sentiments were at that time, the system under the Articles was beginning to show its ineffectiveness. The nascent republic needed some manner of central control to consolidate its monetary system, fund itself through taxation, and consolidate itself as a country in general. Shays' Rebellion would bring that point home, making it clear that the US would have to enact certain reforms if it became a union in the true sense of the word.

When Daniel Shays came home from the war after he had done his part to win America's independence, he was owed money, and he wasn't the only one. Many veterans like him came home hoping to live out the rest of their lives in peace, tending to their farms and enjoying their hard-won liberties. Instead, they found indebted states, each of them individually burdened with the debts incurred during the war. Shays also found that many rural folks like him were personally in debt, often with hefty mortgages hanging over their heads.

As the courts summoned more and more debtors, handed down payment orders, and foreclosed people's properties, dissatisfaction escalated. Many of the targeted farmers were veterans of the

Revolutionary War and firm believers in the founding ideas of liberty in America. To these trained and seasoned veterans of the revolution, the situation they found at home became increasingly reminiscent of the tyranny they once fought. Once again, the independent-minded Americans in the countryside murmured of taxation without representation and recalled the fundamental views of the founding fathers, which held that every free man could and should revolt against all tyranny.

Once Daniel Shays decided to take direct action, he found that assembling a mob of like-minded veterans wasn't too difficult. Everything began with an assembly of farmers in the summer of 1786, which first tried to petition the state of Massachusetts to tone down its crackdown. They demanded a one-year moratorium on tax collection to provide relief to the indebted farmers. They also wanted courts to be suspended to prevent them from confiscating more property. They also wanted more currency to be put into circulation so as to trigger a certain level of inflation, allowing the farmers to make more hard cash from their animals and produce.

These demands received a cold welcome. As a further aggravation, the farmers were smeared as traitors working for the British, despite many of them having participated in the revolution. The merchants and other citizens who had outstanding loans to the farmers pressed the legislature and denounced all petitions, insisting that all debts be repaid in short order. In their minds, the farmers simply had to manage and improvise where necessary to make good on their obligations. Faced with this response, the farmers soon moved on to plan B, which was to arm themselves and use force to blockade the courts.

After a period of strategizing and plotting, the armed bands began to descend on the courts in August. By the end of the month, they besieged and captured the courthouse in Northampton. When the judges attempted to relocate their proceedings to another court, they were met with bayonets. By late September, multiple courthouses were similarly shut down. Around this time, Daniel Shays led a rebel force of around 1,500 men, blocking even the Massachusetts Supreme Court in Springfield. The authorities struggled to assemble the militias to put down the rebellion since many of the would-be militiamen were locals with sympathies to Daniel Shays and the rebel cause.

Although the uprising relied on limited violent actions and produced few casualties, the situation threatened to escalate. At the forefront of such concerns was the massive Springfield Armory. This federal armory was a key production and storage center for the federal arsenal, housing around 7,000 guns and various other weapons, including artillery and substantial amounts of gunpowder. With the terrifying prospect of rebels seizing these weapons looming, Secretary of War Henry Knox called on Congress to deploy federal troops to crush the insurrection. Although his request was granted, the federal government's weakness was demonstrated when it proved unable to muster significant forces.

James Bowdoin.[2]

The job thus fell to Massachusetts Governor James Bowdoin. In his subsequent speech to the state legislature in October, one of the key factors in the ongoing struggle was made apparent. Bowdoin decried the "wicked and artful men" who were hard at work in their attempts to "destroy all confidence in government." Such a declaration made it clear that putting down the insurrection was a matter of consolidating the union and asserting control. Still, the rebels received a minor concession in the form of a temporary suspension of debt payments and foreclosures.

At the same time, the Massachusetts legislature passed the Riot Act and the Militia Act, which were measures meant to crack down on the armed and violent component of the uprising. These acts gave extensive authority to sheriffs to employ harsh, repressive measures against any individuals refusing to cease their participation in mutinies and armed groups. The authorities could use lethal force and summarily confiscate land from rebels while, on the flip side, amnesty was offered to anyone willing to abandon the rebellion.

A minor lull ensued, during which courts went into recess while many farmers returned home for the harvest, but tensions resumed in late autumn. As 1787 began, the governor started assembling a militia of over 4,000 men at arms, financed privately. General Benjamin Lincoln, himself a veteran of the American Revolution, was given command of around 2,000 men and a mandate to restore order across the rural areas of western Massachusetts. The organization of the militias ensured that the rebels could not get their hands on the Springfield Armory, thus potentially preventing a lot of carnage.

Although the state had come to this impasse due to economic hardships and political corruption, the standoff, in its essence, was one between patriots. Shays and his followers believed they were following in the footsteps of the revolution, once again standing up to a detached tyrannical regime. After all, the founding fathers believed that the people had the right and even a duty to overthrow such a regime. To that end, the rebels seized the roads to Springfield and cut off the supply of the militias protecting the armory, courthouse, and other institutions as they prepared for a showdown.

On the other side, those who stood against the insurrection were also guided by patriotism and the belief in America's revolution. For those actively serving the government, collecting taxes was necessary to preserve the country that the founding fathers had established. Nipping the insurrection in the bud was also a matter of precedent, as its failure and the subsequent strengthening of the government would discourage future revolts and empower the forces of order. As for the lenders, their insistence on collecting the debt might have seemed like pure self-interest, but their demands for contracts to be honored were really a matter of property rights, a sacred principle and core value of the United States.

After sending several ultimatums to the defenders in Springfield, Shays' rebel army, numbering around 2,000 men, marched on the armory on January 25, 1787. The militias had established artillery positions to break the assault, but their first volley was fired as a warning, well above the advancing farmers. When the rebels pressed on, the militia shot to kill. The barrage killed four men and wounded many more, which finally forced Shays' men to disperse. Most of the rebel army went home shortly thereafter, while Daniel Shays and some of his inner circle ran to New York and Vermont to hide. A number of high-profile insurrectionists were soon arrested and sentenced to death on charges of treason, but they were eventually pardoned along with Daniel Shays.

The Whiskey Rebellion

Shays' Rebellion might have been crushed, but the underlying problems that precipitated it would persist, as would the government's desperate need to finance itself. More importantly, the Articles of Confederation were still firmly in place and would remain as such until March of 1789, leaving the government chronically inept and ineffective. Despite unresolved issues in both governance and economics, the test of Shays was one that the young union passed.

Americans proved that they cared about the union enough to preserve it and were mature enough to discuss its future order, even though the discussion sometimes got violent. Shays' short-lived rebellion was a signal to many that things needed to change and that the government must be strengthened, which meant reconsidering the Articles. Without a stronger national government, nobody could guarantee that the republic would survive future challenges similar to those presented by Shays. When the form of government under the Articles of Confederation was revised in 1789, the federal government under the Constitution of the United States took its place. The new government featured a strong executive position, which was the president, and it established new courts and granted more taxation powers to the government. The reform was just in time, too, as a new challenge loomed over the horizon.

The Whiskey Rebellion was the only instance in history where a sitting American president led troops into battle, or at least a potential one that was ultimately de-escalated before spiraling out of control. However, the event's historical legacy extends far beyond this interesting bit of trivia. Also, like the insurrection led by Daniel Shays, the Whiskey Rebellion didn't produce a lot of casualties, but it was a landmark event in that it marked the first time the federal government attempted to tax a domestic product in the United States.

The controversial whiskey tax was introduced in 1791 after a proposal by the Secretary of the Treasury and staunch Federalist Alexander Hamilton. After the United States Constitution was ratified in 1789 and the new federal government was formed, the issue of the day continued to be debt. Current debts included some $54 million incurred by the government under the Articles, plus a total of $25 million owed individually by states. This massive debt presented an opportunity for Hamilton to promote the Federalist agenda and consolidate the union.

The first step was constructing a financial system that would pursue prosperity through national unity. The first practical proposal by Hamilton was to join the federal and state debts into one, which came into effect in 1790.

Hamilton knew that the country needed more sources of revenue to handle this debt and other government operations, as he felt that income from imports couldn't be raised any further. This was how Hamilton arrived at the idea of imposing a tax on spirits distilled in the United States, particularly whiskey. President Washington was initially skeptical of Hamilton's proposal, but after touring through Virginia and Pennsylvania, the president's mind was changed by local government officials who supported the tax.

Between the introduction of the tax in 1791 and the eruption of the open rebellion in 1794, there was a period of intense confrontation and ever-escalating violence in response to the tax. This period would impose a pivotal test for the rapidly consolidating federal government, now with a ratified constitution. If the government could impose its authority and prove its ability to garner revenue through taxation, it would set one of the most essential building blocks for the state's future work. Expectedly, there was no shortage of challengers to such a proposition.

The lead-up to the armed revolt in western Pennsylvania featured violent but rarely deadly clashes between opponents and tax collectors. Small whiskey producers initially resorted to protests and laid out their case against the tax, with arguments containing quite a bit of merit. Most contentious was the fact that major producers who could churn out much more liquor enjoyed annual tax rates that featured tax breaks that only increased the more they produced. Most of these large producers paid six cents on the gallon, with a possibility to pay even less if they increased production.

Alexander Hamilton.[3]

10

Meanwhile, small local distilleries and family businesses had a fixed rate of nine cents per gallon. Another major problem for small producers was that taxes could only be paid in cash. This was a problem because much of the farmlands' economy still revolved around bartering, and the farmers were used to paying their obligations in agricultural products, animals, and especially whiskey. Whiskey would not spoil like beer, was easy to transport, and was widely available. More than just a lifeline for the farmers, whiskey often functioned as a form of currency.

Protests by the farmers went unheard, but so did the government's demands for taxation. Locals would often ignore their obligations or use intimidation against tax collectors. With little recourse, the officials could do little to impose the tax on defiant locals, many more than capable of violence. During the period of gradual escalation, tarring and feathering of unwanted officials and taxmen became the go-to tactic for the farmers. Far from the comical and cartoony inconvenience it's sometimes regarded as in popular culture, tarring was a grueling ordeal that caused significant physical pain and psychological trauma to the victims.

This fate notably befell an excise officer named Robert Johnson on September 11, 1791, marking the first major incident of tarring. Disguised as women, eleven men ambushed him in western Pennsylvania, forced him naked, and then drenched him in hot tar and feathers. The man was then left in the forest. One of the men sent to arrest a couple of the identified perpetrators, John Connor, was given the same treatment, only he was bound to a tree and left in the forest for hours. In the coming years, opponents of the tax used increasingly bold and violent methods, breaking into homes and forming mobs that assaulted officials and even their families.

Tensions escalated to new heights through the summer of 1794, as federal marshal David Lenox was preparing to enforce the tax on 60 farmers who had refused to pay. He was joined on July 14 by John Neville, who was a tax collector and wealthy landowner sympathetic to the government's taxation effort. He also had intimate knowledge of Allegheny County in western Pennsylvania, so he offered to act as a guide for Lenox. The following day, the two men went on their official business, first paying a visit to one William Miller, a distiller who had ignored his summons. It wasn't long until the government men were face to face with an angry mob, brandishing muskets and waving pitchforks. The mob was further aggravated by false rumors that federal agents were forcibly taking farmers into custody, but Lenox and Neville were able to de-escalate the situation and leave the area.

On July 16, however, a new mob descended on Neville's home at the Bower Hill mansion, demanding that Lenox surrender into their custody. Following a brief argument, Neville opened fire on the intruders after they refused to leave his property, killing one of the men in the crowd. A volley of fire ensued as Neville's slaves defended the premises, wounding a number of insurrectionists and forcing them to retreat. Enraged by the casualties, the rebels regrouped in the evening and recruited more sympathizers while also designing their own rebel flag.

The next day, a rebel army of around 700 men marched to Bower Hill, outnumbering the ten soldiers that had been assigned to protect Neville's compound. Although Neville had evacuated the mansion and gone into hiding, the soldiers refused to surrender. The rebels allowed the women to vacate the premises before they commenced torching a number of buildings, including the slaves' quarters. They fired on the mansion and engaged the soldiers in an extended firefight, which resulted in the death of James McFarlane, the apparent rebel leader. When McFarlane fell, the rebels intensified their efforts to burn the whole place down, at which point the soldiers surrendered.

Following their pyrrhic victory, the rebels began hearing rumors that Washington was preparing to deploy a militia to crush them. Another wealthy landowner from western Pennsylvania, David Bradford, was sympathetic to the insurrection. He intercepted some letters coming out of Pittsburgh, which seemed to condemn the insurrection. This made it easy for Bradford to rally thousands more men for a preemptive attack on the city, which was meant to get the rebels ahead of George Washington's allegedly impending attack. Around 7,000 armed men then marched to Pittsburgh, but through clever diplomacy and some generosity in the form of whiskey, the city was able to convince the rebels not to attack.

At this time, Hamilton advocated sending troops to Pennsylvania for a decisive response, but Washington preferred giving diplomacy a chance. His attempts at peaceful negotiations failed, so the Supreme Court eventually authorized military action. Washington amassed an enormous, well-armed militia of around 12,000 men from a number of states, including the eastern parts of Pennsylvania. As luck would have it, the situation had apparently begun resolving by the time Washington led his army to a meeting with the rebel representatives.

The rebels assured him that order was being restored and that there was no need for a crackdown. To be sure, the president marched the militia through the countryside, drawing a lot of dirty looks but encountering no armed resistance. A few suspected rebels were apprehended and tried, but most of them were innocent. Even the two that were convicted were eventually pardoned by the president. Things turned out very well for the government in the end. What could have been a bloody, gruesome affair turned out to be a mere test for the new federal government and the Constitution. This was a test that the United States had certainly passed. Difficulties in collecting the whiskey task persisted, though, and it was eventually abandoned in the early 1800s.

The Hartford Convention

At the time of the Hartford Convention in 1814 and 1815, concerns regarding the growing power of government and the persistent economic hardships in New England were exacerbated by an ongoing war with Britain. The War of 1812, which lasted until February 17, 1815, caused significant damage to the economy of New England, but this was simply adding fuel to the fire following grievances against the federal government in the years prior. Particularly vocal were the New England representatives of the Federalist Party, who convened on multiple occasions between December 15, 1814, and January 5, 1815. These meetings in Hartford, Connecticut, where various problems that the Federalists had with the war and the government were discussed, came to be known as the Hartford Convention.

Although the controversial convention passed no resolutions aimed at secession from the union, it's likely that the matter was at least discussed to an extent. While the convention ultimately didn't break up the United States, it was an important landmark in further developing and adapting American federalism. It also marked the beginning of a major decline for the Federalist Party and its influence in American politics, in part owing to their opposition to the war.

The meetings were held in secret and featured delegates from different parts of the US, including Rhode Island, Massachusetts, New Hampshire, Connecticut, and Vermont. Grievances against President James Madison were the focal point. The War of 1812, referred to by many delegates as Mr. Madison's War, was an important part of the deliberations, but it wasn't the only source of dissatisfaction with the president. In the grand scheme of things, the balance of power in the

United States was one of the key points of debate. Many of the delegates had a particular problem with Virginia, which they saw as having too much sway over the federal government.

President James Madison.'

Many of the discussions held at the Hartford Convention had the potential to tear at the fabric of the union. It demonstrated that, even in the 1810s, the United States was still a fragile republic with a considerable way to go toward cementing its cohesion. The delegates could generally be separated into two main camps. The extremist camp suggested that secession from the United States might be the correct course. On the other hand, moderates wanted to amend the Constitution and protect their interest within the confines of the union. It all came to an end with the emphasis on states' rights, which remains one of the cornerstones of American political life. Specifically, the convention passed a series of resolutions that mostly criticized the government's conscription and market regulation policies, finalizing the writings on January 4, 1815.

The Hartford Convention's main blunder was that it convened just as some of its biggest grievances were being resolved. For instance, a British ship carrying the terms of peace concluded in the Treaty of Ghent crossed the Atlantic before the convention finalized its resolutions. The plan was to bring the reports and resolutions of the convention to Washington and submit them as terms, but before the convention's emissaries arrived at the capital, they learned of a major American victory in the Battle of New Orleans.

The ultimatum that the convention sought to present to the government had thus become obsolete, as much of the crisis that precipitated the convention had begun to subside. In the end, the Hartford Convention's only notable achievement was to discredit itself and the Federalists as a whole once the public caught wind of the secrecy surrounding the meetings. The delegates came across as schemers, scurrying around in the shadows while the army fought battles against the British. Had the war been lost, perhaps the convention's arguments would have received more credit, but the war's inconclusive end seemed to satisfy much of the country, and people were ready to move on. The convention was cast aside and frowned upon, contributing to the eventual fall of the Federalist Party.

Recap Questions

- How did economic difficulties in the post-Revolutionary period catalyze both Shay's and the Whiskey Rebellion?

_____

_____

_____

_____

- Why was the Whiskey Rebellion a pivotal moment for the federal government's authority?

_____

_____

_____

_____

- In what ways did the Hartford Convention represent the ideological divides in early America?

_____

_____

_____

_____

Chapter 2: Race and Ethnicity – The Nation's Struggles

Throughout American history, one of the hottest topics has been the omnipresent issue of race relations. Unfortunately, America's struggle with adapting to its inherent diversity has been a cultural, economic, and institutional problem that persists today. The United States has undoubtedly come a very long way in this regard, but centuries of strife and oppression have left residual effects that are difficult to deracinate.

A Jim Crow sign in the US.[5]

A lot of these scars are the result of misguided policies and failings in the justice system of the US, comprising several historic mistakes and legislative blunders that have left a deep impact on American racial dynamics. Court rulings and discriminatory laws targeting racial or ethnic groups were major features of the American experience on numerous occasions. Not only did they cause tremendous damage in their day, but these measures and injustices have profoundly affected future generations, sociopolitical dynamics, and the American mentality as a whole.

The Dred Scott Decision

The Dred Scott decision refers to the events surrounding a landmark Supreme Court ruling in the case of *Dred Scott v. Sandford* in 1856-1857. This historic case and its decision perfectly exemplify an entire zeitgeist of prejudice and injustice toward African Americans in the gradual lead-up to the American Civil War. Even though progressive thinking and abolitionist movements gained traction throughout the 19th century, the legal system would take quite a while to catch up. This was a time when the United States legal system not only deprived Blacks of fundamental rights like citizenship but outright disaffirmed their status as human beings. The case of Dred Scott was emblematic of all the evils of slavery, racial discrimination, and emerging counterforces of the day.

Dred Scott's story was a ten-year struggle that took him through numerous courts before his case reached the Supreme Court. In essence, this man's struggle was a fight to prove to the United States that he was a man as opposed to another man's property. This fundamental truth was one that Scott could not effectively communicate to his country, as the system would ultimately rule against him. As disheartening as it was, the legal system's complete failure by all human metrics carried a hidden victory, as the story of Dred Scott accelerated America's long-overdue shift away from slavery.

Scott was born sometime around 1799 as a slave in Southampton County, Virginia. He was owned by Peter Blow throughout his early life, relocating multiple times between 1818 and 1830 in the company of his owner. These travels saw Scott living as a slave in Missouri and Alabama for certain periods. Scott's first owner died in 1832, after which he was sold to Dr. John Emerson, a US Army surgeon. As before, Scott would travel and relocate frequently with his master, but with Emerson, some of these travels were to free states such as Illinois and Wisconsin

Territory. In Wisconsin, Scott would spend some time at Fort Snelling, where he went on to marry Harriet Robinson, herself also a slave. Harriet's owner didn't object to the marriage and even transferred her to Emerson so she could be with her husband.

Slowly but surely, Dred Scott began tasting freedom, even though he was legally a slave. When Emerson left for St. Louis in 1837, he left Scott and Harriet behind, letting them be hired by others while living their lives as a couple. The main chapter in Dred Scott's tale began shortly after that – when Emerson moved to Louisiana, where he met and married Eliza Irene Sanford. After the wedding in February 1838, Emerson invited Dred and Harriet to join him in Louisiana. After they reunited, Emerson's family and their slaves once again relocated to Wisconsin. Over the next few years, Dred and Harriet continued living with Emerson and had two daughters.

Following Emerson's honorable discharge from the army in 1842, there were a couple more relocations before Emerson's unexpected death in 1843 while living in Iowa. This meant that Scott and his family, along with other slaves owned by Emerson, became the property of his wife Irene. Irene soon moved to St. Louis and left her slaves behind to be hired out, but she had no intention of setting them free. It was around this time that Dred Scott's dream of freeing himself and his family from bondage was undoubtedly crystallized in his mind. The first course he tried was to buy his freedom from Irene, but his offers were turned down.

In 1846, both Dred and Harriet tried their luck with the legal system, filing two separate lawsuits at the St. Louis Circuit Court, suing Irene for their freedom. One of the statutes the Scotts relied upon in their case was a Missouri statute that envisioned automatic freedom for any slave entering a free territory, which Scott and his wife had done plenty of times. Unfortunately, the Scotts were both illiterate and needed extensive help navigating the court's complicated affairs. Their church, sympathetic volunteers, and even the Blow family, which had previously owned Dred Scott, pitched in to help.

The first trial, which began on June 30, 1847, didn't end in the Scotts' favor, but the judge promptly allowed a retrial. The initial ruling was based on a technicality, as the court had argued that the Scotts couldn't prove that Irene even owned them. Another trial was held in early 1850, which ended with a ruling that granted the Scotts their freedom.

Unfortunately, this twist of good fortune was to be short-lived as Irene quickly appealed the decision at the Missouri Supreme Court. The Supreme Court reversed the decision in 1852, and the Scott family still found themselves in slavery. It was probably around this time that Irene transferred the Scotts to the ownership of her brother, John Sanford.

Scott decided to take his case federal in November of 1853, suing John Sanford for his freedom at the US Circuit Court for the District of Missouri. The federal lawsuit brought a lot more attention to Scott's predicament in a country that was already increasingly divided on the subject of slavery. Unfortunately, the court ruled against Scott on May 15, 1854, but this was just the beginning. In December of that year, Scott decided to appeal the decision, this time at the United States Supreme Court. It took a while before the trial commenced in February of 1856, but the entrance of the case into the highest court in the land garnered more attention and controversy than ever before.

Major abolitionist activists, sympathetic politicians, and high-end lawyers all expressed an interest and offered their help as the case gradually turned into something much greater than itself. At the US Supreme Court, the case against John Sanford became *Dred Scott v. Sandford* due to a clerk's error, entering historical records with the defendant's name misspelled. To the dismay of Scott and many hopeful opponents of slavery, Scott lost the case on March 6, 1857. The Supreme Court's final ruling explained that even hearing Scott's case had been unconstitutional, as he was not a citizen but property.

Chief Justice Roger Taney's final majority opinion, rather eloquent in its infamy, explained that no African-Americans, freemen and slaves alike, could be a citizen. As such, Americans of African descent had no right to use federal courts. Furthermore, the opinion implied that it was Sanford whose rights were under attack, particularly his property rights, as per the Fifth Amendment. In Taney's words, the court opined that legislation, history, and even the Declaration of Independence clearly showed that neither the original imported slaves nor their descendants – freed or not – were "acknowledged as a part of the people."

Needless to say, Taney was widely vilified among a sizeable part of the population that had already lost its stomach for slavery. The cruel ruling and the final opinion probably turned a lot of fence-sitters against the evils of slavery as well. More importantly, the ruling was interpreted as an attempt to prevent future debate about abolition due to its broad-stroke dismissal of all African Americans and their claims to freedom, let alone citizenship. The Dred Scott decision certainly didn't end slavery, but it was a major stepping stone toward galvanizing the abolitionist movement and deepening the divide in the United States. Unfortunately, that divide wasn't destined to be solved in conversation. Instead, it led to the formation of the Confederate States of America, secession, and a gruesome civil war following the 1862 Emancipation Proclamation.

Also emblematic of the heated sociopolitical atmosphere at the time was the twist of fate that ultimately won Dred Scott his freedom. Before Scott's case was concluded, Irene had remarried with Calvin Chaffee, a congressman and sympathizer of the abolitionist cause. Seeing the hypocrisy in having anything to do with Scott's enslavement, Chaffee soon sold the entire Scott family to Taylor Blow. Taylor was the son of Scott's original owner, Peter Blow. Deciding to do what his father had never gotten around to, Taylor freed the Scotts on May 26, 1857.

Dred Scott.[6]

As a free man, Scott worked in St. Louis and would only enjoy his freedom for a little over a year before dying from tuberculosis on September 17, 1858. He left behind a free wife and children and an immense legacy, having inspired countless abolitionists at the time and many human rights advocates ever since. Dred Scott's plight also greatly inspired Harriet Beecher Stowe's famous novel, *Uncle Tom's Cabin.* Apart from being a source of inspiration, Dred Scott's story still stands as one of the most despicable moments in the history of the US justice system.

The Indian Removal Act

Andrew Jackson's Indian Removal Act of 1830 was one of the pivotal moments in the earlier stages of American westward expansion. It was a dreadful microcosm of a lot of the injustices inflicted upon the Natives in those days, in this case, signed into law and executed in a highly organized, state-sanctioned manner. The act and the subsequent forced relocation of the so-called Five Civilized Tribes and other Native groups precipitated the infamous Trail of Tears.

The official stated goal was an exchange of land with the Indians and their relocation to allotted federal land west of the Mississippi. The seizure of highly desirable lands east of the river, occupied at that time by Indian territories within several states, was the true objective of President Jackson and his supporters. However, the initiative was often portrayed as being part of an effort to "civilize" Native Americans and integrate them into the United States. There was also an element of misguided altruism in the explanation that the Natives were receiving supposedly valuable federal land in the form of reservations.

In reality, the lands that the Natives inhabited east of the Mississippi were fertile, quality real estate that White settlers wanted to appropriate. Across Georgia, Alabama, North Carolina, Florida, and Tennessee, millions of acres were inhabited by some 125,000 Natives belonging to the five tribes. These Natives had lived there for generations, but their lands were needed for cotton production, and so the wheels were set in motion. It would take less than a decade through the 1830s to turn the Natives in the southeastern United States into a tiny minority within the realm of statistical error.

In a way, the Indian Removal Act was also a story of great betrayal when contrasted with the background of the Five Civilized Tribes. The friction between the Natives and White people – European colonizers and their American descendants after them – was long-standing and well-understood. The concept behind the Five Civilized Tribes was born of early attempts by the federal government to solve the apparent "Indian problem" through assimilation. This was the preferred method of George Washington, who made great efforts to motivate the Choctaw, Chickasaw, Seminole, Creek, and Cherokee tribes to adopt the ways of the White man. This meant learning English at American schools, accepting Christianity, adopting American-style concepts of property, and much more. In some instances, the "civilized" Natives even owned slaves in the South. Unfortunately for the Indians, assimilating into White America would ultimately not be enough to preserve their presence in the land.

The Indian Removal Act was simply the final chapter in a prolonged period of violence and terror that the Natives in the southeast suffered at the hands of settlers. Land seizures, theft, looting, arson, and other injustices had gone on for years, but the 1830 act would legitimize with government backing the previously sporadic efforts to drive the Natives out. President Jackson's act was often supplemented by individual states through their own laws to speed up the process. The Supreme Court would intervene a few times against the more egregious instances, but there was no stopping the overall tide.

Located in present-day Oklahoma, the western lands meant for the Natives were merely an offer on paper. The Indian Removal Act had provisions that limited the methods the government could use to relocate the Indians, not allowing coercion and violence. Removals were supposed to be negotiated fairly, resulting in voluntary, peaceful relocation. In practice, these stipulations were little more than letters on a piece of paper.

Already in late 1831, the Choctaw tribe was threatened by the US Army, which was poised to invade and expel them after failed negotiations. Poorly supplied and with no help from the government, the Natives were forced to make the long journey to new territories on foot. Thousands died in what the Choctaw described as a "trail of tears and death." Over the next few years, the same fate befell the other tribes. Members of some tribes, like the Cherokee, advocated armed resistance, but most knew this would be a suicidal cause.

Instead, some members of the tribe took it upon themselves to negotiate, without authority, the controversial 1835 Treaty of New Echota. The government was quick to take this deal, which gave millions of acres of Indian land in exchange for $5 million, other compensation, and government assistance in relocation. The treaty was treated as illegitimate and a fraud by the majority of the tribe and their leader, John Ross. A huge assembly of Cherokee petitioned the government not to legitimize the treaty, but it went through Congress anyway. Unwilling to accept what they felt was a government scam, most of the Cherokee stayed on their land.

This defiance led to a crackdown in 1838 when President Martin Van Buren sent an army to forcibly drive the Natives out. The troops drove the Cherokee from their homes with bayonets, looted their towns, and pressed them into a 1,200-mile march to their new lands. The conditions during the long march were horrendous, once again leading to thousands of deaths due to disease outbreaks, starvation, and much more. Historiography now refers to the Trail of Tears as a decade-long process involving numerous routes, more than 5,000 miles across nine states. In the end, not even the so-called Indian Territory would be left untouched as American settlements kept inching westward. By the early 1900s, the territory became increasingly smaller and was eventually incorporated as the state of Oklahoma. Only in the 21ˢᵗ century did the Supreme Court begin correcting some of these wrongs, restoring the Indian reservation over a significant chunk of the state.

The Chinese Exclusion Act

The Chinese Exclusion Act of 1882 was another regrettable episode in American race relations, notable as the first major federal law that restricted immigration, in this case, specifically along ethnic lines. The act was born of relatively widespread sentiments at the time. It was a reflection of America's broader views regarding immigration in the 19ᵗʰ century, especially concerning labor. The demands to curtail Chinese immigration came mostly from workers, resulting from a decline in wages and other economic issues. Many workers blamed these struggles on foreign workers from China – who were perceived as driving down wages because of their willingness to work for less and take over valuable jobs.

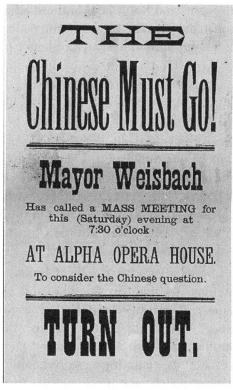

The Chinese Must Go poster in 1885.[7]

To what extent these fears were rooted in reality is debatable since the Chinese comprised a minuscule fraction of America's population at the time, amounting to around 0.002%. Regardless of the true factors at play in America's economic hardships, the sentiment against the Chinese was pervasive enough to exert significant pressure on Congress to do something about it. Amid the controversy, supporters of such an act who were motivated primarily by race and not by labor concerns also participated in the campaign, pursuant to their goal of keeping America racially homogeneous.

The reason for the notable increase of Chinese immigration to the US during the 19ᵗʰ century had everything to do with China's own difficult historical episode at that time. Following the Opium Wars with the British around the middle of the century and destructive internal turmoil as the last imperial dynasty declined, China was indebted, chaotic, and incredibly poor. Making matters worse were natural disasters such as droughts and floods. All of these afflictions made China almost unlivable for many peasants in the countryside, leading many of them to make the long trips abroad in search of better prospects.

After gold was discovered in the Sacramento Valley in 1848, the ensuing California Gold Rush triggered the first big wave of Chinese immigration to the US. The influx intensified in 1852 when more than 20,000 new immigrants entered through San Francisco, and it wasn't long until racial intolerance and stiff labor competition led to conflict with White miners in the state. The Chinese were initially encouraged to immigrate as the Gold Rush had produced an insatiable demand for laborers. The demand only grew when the Chinese proved themselves to be reliable workers. The US and China eventually engaged in free trade, allowing a free flow of Chinese workers into America from 1868 following the Burlingame Treaty.

Soon after arriving, the Chinese were doing much more than just mining, as their work ethic and skills were sought after in railway construction projects and other sectors essential to sustaining American endeavors in the frontier lands. Beyond manual labor, the Chinese immigrants also demonstrated an entrepreneurial spirit, opening restaurants, laundries, stores, and various other small businesses. Unfortunately, the more success that they found in America, the more they were seen as a threat by a significant portion of American society. The first legislative response to the immigration influx was the Foreign Miners License Tax, which California aimed specifically at Chinese miners. It wasn't long until frictions intensified, and things began getting very violent, with attacks on Chinese immigrants becoming increasingly common.

The unfair treatment of the Chinese immigrants by the justice system contributed immensely to the violence because it all but encouraged attacks. Following some controversial legal proceedings at the California Supreme Court in the mid-1850s, it became apparent that Chinese immigrants, just like African Americans and Natives, could not be used as witnesses in court, especially against Whites. What this meant in practice is that the Chinese effectively had no legal protection against violence, which was becoming disturbingly common. In the coming years, despite their deplorable legal status, Chinese workers continued their labor while bringing millions of dollars in revenue to the government through the Foreign Miners License Tax. In 1870, the government had made $5 million from these taxes, all while the Chinese were being attacked and systematically discriminated against daily.

By this time, anti-Chinese sentiment among workers in California took on the shape of a statewide movement. Even though the Chinese made up a tiny fraction of America's overall population, the influx of immigrants created significant local Chinese communities on the West Coast. As these populations grew in the second half of the 19th century, the Chinese also proved themselves to be highly capable miners, which unfortunately only exacerbated the intolerance against them. Before the Chinese Exclusion Act was ever enacted, disgruntled locals had already begun pressuring the Chinese away from the gold-mining areas, forcing many of them to relocate to San Francisco. In the city, they could do little more than exhausting, menial labor for very low wages.

In the lead-up to the act, the Chinese were consistently slandered and subjected to all sorts of racially-charged propaganda. They were portrayed as dangerous foreigners, but labor competition was always at the heart of the issue. This was exemplified perfectly by statements made by Senator John F. Miller, one of the key supporters of the act. He described the Chinese as "machine-like," almost immune to heat or cold, and with muscles of iron. Such statements were anything but flattering, however, as their true motive was to stigmatize Chinese workers as unfairly advantaged and destructive to the American labor market. These stereotypes were instrumental in helping labor organizations push for anti-Chinese legislation, with the primary goal being at least a temporary ban on further Chinese immigration.

By all indications, the movement was a grassroots effort originating in widespread sentiments. Some scholars have since argued that the initiative came from the top, encouraged by politicians to stoke the flames and win votes. However, this would have been difficult to accomplish without a preexisting, spontaneous emergence of prejudice in the wider population. Indeed, anti-Chinese sentiment has been widely described as an endemic feature of American culture and sociopolitical dynamics at that time, at least on the West Coast.

Popular demand ultimately won, and the government responded. When the Chinese Exclusion Act was finally signed by President Chester A. Arthur, its original idea was to stop Chinese immigration for ten years. The act also stipulated that Chinese immigrants could no longer be naturalized, barring those who had already immigrated from citizenship. After the act became law on May 6, 1882, there were some efforts to shoot it down as unconstitutional, but to no avail. However, the 1882 act was just the beginning and would be further amended in the coming years to become even more restrictive.

The Chinese Exclusion Act, along with its subsequent amendments, did much more than prevent new Chinese immigrants from coming into the United States. In many ways, the legislation made life more difficult for the Chinese already living in America while also making deportations easier. For instance, leaving America and coming back would become increasingly difficult until it eventually became impossible. Initially, Chinese-American men could only reenter the US with a special certification. The act was amended in 1884 to make reentry even harder regardless of the country of origin, as the Chinese were excluded from all possibility of becoming citizens.

In 1888, the Scott Act upgraded the Chinese Exclusion Act, which banned reentry altogether, with some exceptions provided for teachers, government officials, merchants, and a few other groups. This meant that no regular Chinese worker in America could ever go back to China to visit their relatives without being permanently banned from the United States. The controversial 1889 case of *Chae Chan Ping v. United States* directly resulted from this problem. Ping wasn't even aware of how strict the anti-Chinese provisions had become in his absence when he tried to return to the US after visiting his folks in China.

A SKELETON IN HIS CLOSET.

A cartoon showing Uncle Sam protesting against the Russian exclusion of Jewish Americans while being confronted with the American exclusion of the Chinese.'

Shocked that he was prohibited from entering a country where he had built his life, Ping tried to challenge the acts and eventually took his case to the Supreme Court. Both the Chinese Exclusion Act and the Scott Act were upheld as constitutional and then extended for another ten years via the Geary Act of 1892. The Geary Act also stipulated that Chinese residents would have to possess special documents to be carried on their person at all times. These were residential certificates issued by the IRS, and failing to produce the document for inspection in any instance would result in prosecution. After sentencing, these residents would either be sent to hard labor or immediately deported, with no bail possible unless the accused Chinaman could summon a White witness to vouch for them.

In all these years, the only positive development in the status of Chinese Americans was that they were allowed to testify in court from 1882 onward. In all other areas, they would only find fewer and fewer rights as the years went on. Each time a Chinese American was prevented from reentering America, much more than their freedom of movement was violated. Apart from breaking up families, the anti-Chinese acts violated the fundamental property rights of Chinese people whenever reentry was denied, cutting them off from everything they earned and owned in America after years of hard work.

These discriminatory laws remained popular for a long time, and they were certainly effective, leading to a significant decline in America's Chinese population. The 20th century only brought further restrictions, with all Chinese immigration permanently banned in 1902. The measures also provided a precedent and framework for future legislative efforts to limit or prohibit immigration from specific countries and ethnic groups, which continued well into the years of World War II. All the Chinese people still living in America, many of them born there, would have to wait until the 1943 Magnuson Act for a chance to get their citizenship. The act was likely a move to placate China amid America's war with Japan and the need to form alliances in Asia, although the alliance came naturally since Japan was a terrifying common enemy in those days.

Recap Questions

- How did the Dred Scott Decision exacerbate tensions between the North and the South?

_____

_____

_____

_____

- What economic and territorial motivations underpinned the Indian Removal Act, beyond mere prejudice?

_____

_____

_____

_____

- In what ways did the Chinese Exclusion Act reflect America's broader views on immigration and labor during the late 19th century?

_____

_____

_____

_____

Chapter 3: Early Economic Earthquakes

As a country and culture emphasizing economic liberties and the free market, the United States is no stranger to periodic episodes of economic disruption. Due to the 2008 global financial crisis and the very recent economic downturn in the aftermath of the COVID-19 pandemic, economic hardships are still fresh in memory. Long before that, however, America went through several economic storms that deeply shook the country and vital public perceptions of its financial system.

Unemployment during the great depression.[9]

The country would have to adapt and overcome each time, sometimes through extensive government intervention. Such interventions would sometimes produce mixed results, while in other cases, a lack of willingness on the government's part to step in carried its own problems. This chapter will look at several such episodes, mainly in the late 19ᵗʰ century, the interwar period with the infamous Great Depression, and the dawn of the digital era at the turn of the 21ˢᵗ century. Apart from their economic destructiveness, the significance of America's past financial troubles was and remains in the societal repercussions they wrought and the political and regulatory reforms that each crisis necessitated. As in all other aspects of American life, the country's economic crises have demonstrated America's ability to adapt and reform its systems in response to every challenge.

The Panic of 1893

Well before the infamous economic collapses in the 20ᵗʰ century, the US had another significant encounter with economic depression in the 1890s. The Panic of 1893 and its consequences lasted until 1897 and wreaked havoc across different sectors of the US economy. Apart from the lives it ruined, this depression produced significant political fallout that led to a whole range of ramifications in American politics, particularly regarding regulation. The panic led to the closure of around 15,000 businesses and 500 banks amid a dramatic stock market downturn. The US Treasury was also hit particularly hard, experiencing a troubling decrease in its gold reserves, prompting President Cleveland to borrow from Wall Street. Needless to say, the presidency took major political hits as a result of the crisis.

As with most economic crises in history, the causes of the 1893 panic have long been analyzed and theorized. As always, it's difficult to blame one single culprit among a confluence of factors that came together to form a perfect economic storm. One of the causes often cited had to do with investments in Argentina, a country that experienced crop failures and an attempted coup in 1890, which caused a major upset in foreign investment. The investments were often speculative in nature and encouraged by Baring Brothers, a British merchant bank. Around this time, extensive speculative investments were also injected into South African and Australian properties, which experienced a similar collapse.

These investment instabilities caused concern in a number of European countries that had already entered a period of economic downturn, particularly France, Germany, and England. From 1889, France was already in recession, with business also slowing down in Germany and England shortly after. Uncertainties about the future kicked off a period of gold hoarding and the Europeans' significant selloff of stocks in American companies. All of this triggered a run on gold by European investors in the US Treasury, as paper money was perceived to be less valuable and safe at the time. Specie, or coins made from refined precious metals, was particularly sought after. Simply put, a growing number of investors sought to abandon cash and cash in on their investments to secure their holdings by turning them into gold and specie. All of this made for an all-around climate of economic vulnerability and shaky financing.

Another major factor in the panic was a growing railroad bubble, one of the features of the preceding Gilded Age between the 1870s and 1880s. The Gilded Age refers to a period of expansion and substantial growth in the American economy, which might have been vulnerable growth due to its dependence on high-priced international commodities. When wheat prices crashed in 1893, largely due to the problems in Argentina, the effects on economic growth and investment patterns were significant. The railroad bubble resulted from accelerated building in the 1880s, riding on the waves of the Gilded Age. The more building projects that cropped up, the more lucrative the sector seemed to investors, leading to overbuilding.

Further complicating the situation was an overabundance of silver, which resulted from an exponentially increasing number of mines in the western United States. Many of the people who owned silver wanted to simplify the process of turning the precious metal into money, which led to a widespread debate in the US, carried largely by the Free Silver movement. Miners were particularly interested in driving up the demand for silver, so they wanted to be able to mint silver into currency without a central institution in the middle.

These interest groups found allies among the farmers who sought to put an end to deflation, which was increasing the value of their debts at the time. Opponents wanted the government to stay careful and prevent abundant silver from flooding the market. The 1890 Sherman Silver Purchase Act resulted from the clash of these ideas. It didn't completely liberalize minting but instructed the government to buy much more silver than was required. Silver notes became abundant as a result, and it wasn't long until people started exchanging them for gold.

Federal gold reserves decreased sharply from that point on, and such exchanges were no longer possible once the reserves plummeted to the statutory limit. Once the notes could no longer be redeemed for gold, the demand for silver declined, driving down its value. This and other factors led to bank failures, which caused major railroad companies to fail as well. Bankruptcies became widespread across all sorts of companies from that point on as the panic went into full swing. It became clear that the economy was in trouble on February 20, 1893, just twelve days before Grover Cleveland was supposed to be inaugurated.

Cleveland's first step was to tackle the emerging crisis in the Treasury, which he tried to do by getting Congress to repeal the Sherman Silver Purchase Act. However, this was too little and too late, as the wider public had already caught wind of the trouble ahead. As always, people ran to the banks to salvage their money, wreaking havoc on the financial system. At the same time, a panic occurred in London while trade across Europe decreased – all of which led many European investors to sell off their stocks in American companies.

The Gilded Age was a time of limited financial controls and government intervention in the market. With the 1887 Interstate Commerce Act and the 1890 Sherman Antitrust Act, reformists were able to make some progress toward strengthening government control over business, but the reforms didn't go very far. Thanks to their immense influence, powerful business interests had an easy time making these acts work for them. Antitrust laws, for instance, were meant to break up large monopolies, but in practice, they more often targeted labor unions since the laws were seldom applied to corporate trusts.

Lax government oversight, various financial bubbles, and speculative investment bonanzas at home and abroad during the preceding decades seemed to have brought the chickens home to roost. Although it's often historically overshadowed by the Great Depression, the 1893 panic and its consequences were devastating. The hundreds of banks that went belly up reflected a collapse in public trust in the banking system, and thousands of businesses suffered as a result. In the ensuing depression, the unemployment rate went as high as 43% in some states, with Michigan being hit particularly hard. Starvation became a prevalent problem, with meal centers being set up to feed the hungry. Individuals and families resorted to desperate measures just to survive. In Detroit, Mayor Hazen S. Pingree had to establish community gardens to farm potatoes for the starving.

Mayor Hazen S. Pingree.[10]

Although some scholars have placed considerable blame on the previous policies of President Benjamin Harrison, it was Cleveland who took most of the blame at the time. The government incurred considerable debt to J.P. Morgan and the Rothschild family in an effort to keep the Treasury afloat. All of this led to a political catastrophe for Cleveland's party in the 1894 elections. By 1896, the Democrats were essentially purged from all branches of government after a string of electoral debacles, from which they wouldn't recover until 1910. Various industries suffered great losses, especially shipping and railroad building. The economic collapse also led to unrest, such as the Pullman Strike of 1894, which was crushed by the army.

The Stock Market Crash of 1929

The Wall Street Crash of 1929 is also remembered as the Crash of '29, Black Tuesday, or simply the Great Crash. Given its immense economic fallout, the latter name is perhaps the most fitting description of this monumental financial catastrophe. The Great Crash began in September of 1929, leading to a sudden collapse in share prices on the NY Stock Exchange. This collapse was one of the principal factors that led to the Great Depression, making it America's most horrendous stock market crash to date when all of its implications are considered.

The consequences also lasted for an extended period as the Great Depression eventually took on a global dimension, ruining millions of lives in the process. Putting things in perspective, between 1929 and 1932, the global GDP plummeted by around 15%. This immense downturn dwarfed that of the Great Recession in the late 2000s, which reduced worldwide GDP by less than 1% and still caused extensive damage. The crash of 1929 culminated on October 24 and 29, days remembered as Black Thursday and Black Tuesday, respectively.

The crowning achievement of Wall Street during this calamity was on October 29, when investors traded around 16 million shares at the NYSE in one day. This record-breaking trade volume followed another grim record on October 24, when investors conducted the largest share selloff in American history. The Wall Street crash was also preceded by a similar incident at the London Stock Exchange in September, which is why September is usually regarded as the beginning of the Great Crash.

Similarly to the 1893 panic, the Great Crash followed a period of intense economic activity associated with the so-called Roaring Twenties. During this time of luxury, urbanization, and excess, growth was largely carried by the expansion of the stock market in the United States. The country had recently exited World War I as one of the victorious powers with virtually no damage to itself, earning a seat at the table of major post-war decisions that would determine the future course of the world. The triumphant 1920s were a time of great optimism and excitement, as reflected in the cultural and artistic boom that eventually led to the decade being labeled as "roaring." It was also a period of economic prosperity, which directed a lot of that optimism toward the economy and the financial system.

As always, optimism about the future translated into intensified speculative investment in the stock market. Americans from the rural countryside flocked to the cities, all hoping to get their slice of the seemingly unstoppable growth and prosperity. Unfortunately, the enormous expansion of the stock market, which hit an absolute peak in August of 1929, was a deceptive indicator. Over the years of this apparent growth, production was declining, slowing down the underlying economy beneath the stocks. Stock values were thus exaggerated and inflated dangerously beyond their true value. Wages also stagnated, and they were struggling to keep up, which was one of the reasons debt grew as well. Banks gave out large loans that were difficult or impossible to liquidate. On top of everything else, agriculture was in its own decline, partly due to rapid urbanization as rural populations flocked to the cities.

It was only a matter of time until stock prices would tip over and adjust to the current state of the real economy. That process began gradually in September and continued in early October of 1929. The stock decline escalated on October 18 when a noticeable drop occurred, big enough to set off a panic. Six days later, shareholders traded close to 13 million shares as everyone rushed to get ahead of the collapse, thus aggravating the situation as always.

In the immediate aftermath of the crash, investors and major Wall Street bankers came together to pool their resources and try to keep the market afloat by buying up certain stocks. Richard Whitney coordinated the effort, allocating capital to buying 25,000 shares of US Steel above the market price. Some of the investments went to other companies as well, and the bankers were able to create a temporary rally on Friday. This short-lived respite lasted through the weekend, hailed by many as a "recovery" of the stock market. The *Brooklyn Daily Times* ran a front-page headline saying that stocks are rebounding after the crash. Bankers like Thomas W. Lamont of the Morgan Bank also did their best to reassure the public, calling the crash only a "technical break" and "no cause for alarm."

However, Monday brought the beginning of the next crash, and on Black Tuesday, there was no denying the harsh new reality. Following the record-breaking stock trade that day, some $14 billion in stock value was wiped out. Thousands of investors went completely bust, and most traders were left blind due to the stock tickers lagging behind, unable to handle the trade volume and provide current information. In other words, share prices plummeted faster than anybody could track them!

Following the disaster of October 29, there would be a partial recovery in stock prices, but the overall value continued to decline as the country had already entered the Great Depression. Within three years, the general picture in the market was bleak, with stocks amounting to a measly 20% of the value they had before the Great Crash. The trust in the financial system and the banks was at an all-time low, leading to the failure of around half of all American banks by 1933.

However, the human cost was far worse as the Great Depression remains one of the worst economic calamities to ever hit the world. Unemployment eventually reached 30% across the US, sometimes working in unison with droughts and destructive dust storms across American prairies, parts of which became known as the Dust Bowl. Fleeing complete desolation and starvation, farmers relocated to the cities in search of work, many of them finding equally bleak prospects there. It was only after Franklin D. Roosevelt introduced the radical New Deal in 1933 that some of the Great Depression's worst effects were ameliorated. Controversial to this day, the New Deal was a period of reform that saw extensive government intervention, social programs, and various public projects between 1933 and 1938. As radical as it was, it still took years to produce considerable effects. Even so, it could also be argued that the rapid industrialization precipitated by World War II from 1939 helped finally turn the economy around.

The Dot-com Bubble

Also referred to as the dot-com boom, the dot-com bubble was a stock market event that marked the relatively sudden entrance of the United States into the Information Age, or rather, the proliferation of the Internet. In the late 1990s and around the turn of the century, the stock market experienced a major bubble carried by a saturation of new dot-com startups. The novelty of these online businesses, especially online shopping platforms, incentivized excessive speculative investments of venture capital into Internet startups, resulting in an often unjustified, massive growth in their market valuations.

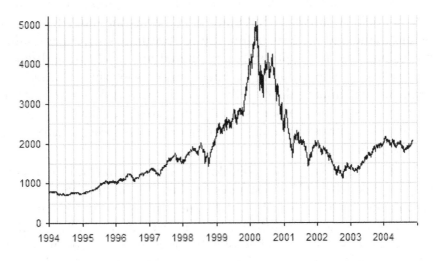

A screenshot of the dot-com bubble event in the late 90s.[11]

The sudden and unsustainable boom made an eventual crash only a matter of time. This particular bubble followed a similar pattern of speculative investment and eventual collapse as the two panics discussed above. In all three cases, the market was allowed to run its course with limited government oversight all the way until disaster struck. All three crashes also followed a period of real or perceived prosperity that incentivized speculative investments. One notable aspect of the dot-com bubble was that the novelty factor behind the speculations was particularly strong.

In the lead-up to the 1893 panic, railroad construction wasn't a new concept, but the period saw an unprecedented explosion in building projects. As the United States sought to expand its infrastructure and consolidate control over its increased territory, the 1870s saw widespread expansion of the railways, and infrastructural projects on that scale did have a degree of novelty, motivating investors to try and get ahead of the future. In the late 1990s, however, the advent of affordable computers and the Internet was novel, creating a true digital gold rush.

The dot-com bubble began around 1995 and peaked on March 10, 2000. The crux of the problem was in the fact that investment was driven primarily by unsubstantiated belief in the guaranteed prosperity of endless Internet startups that cropped up all over the place. Without proper analysis and strategy, many investors were simply struck by the exciting new technology that was being widely adopted by the public. In the context of the late 1990s, it was difficult to predict that online business would go anywhere but upward, and everyone wanted to gain a foothold in the new industry before future growth. Even companies that were making little to no profit, barely offered any products, and didn't even present viable business models could still attract significant investments by simply riding on the wave of the grand new frontier in tech. For many of these businesses, all they needed was clever marketing to attract major investments into their shares and massively grow their market capitalizations.

The banking sector also contributed to the saturation of online startups thanks to low interest rates at the end of the 1990s. Many entrepreneurs with the smallest of business ideas could get attractive loans and register a new company. The massive increase in the number of online businesses was matched only by the lightning speed with which the Internet proliferated in the US. Early in 1993, access to the Internet was unattractive due to technological limitations, but a massive change was just around the corner. When Mosaic came out later that year, users were finally given a viable web browser to surf the World Wide Web, and everything changed.

Connectivity also rapidly improved, and by 1997, computers had shifted from being an unnecessary luxury to an everyday necessity. Within a month of Mosaic's release, Internet traffic was launched into the stratosphere. With cheap loans and the next big technological breakthrough bursting on the scene, a whole new economy materialized before everyone's eyes. Entrepreneurs left and right rushed to get an early start on the shiny new thing and make their historic mark. Simply put, the hype was in the driving seat and was about to usher in a new way of business thinking.

Indeed, as countless new businesses joined the market, they made themselves attractive not based on what they really offered or produced but on promises of what was to come. Thanks to the novelty of the Internet, many investors were willing to abandon traditional modes of thinking about investment and stocks, rushing in on trust rather than careful planning. The untapped potential, which really was there, had a blinding effect on the public. In this climate, Netscape Communications, with their 1994 web browser Navigator, entered the scene and pushed out Mosaic.

Thanks to the hype around new tech, Netscape and similar companies could do the impossible – attract investors without making solid profits. Even though Netscape was constantly losing money, they were able to trigger a gold rush in the stock market. After Netscape went public, its stock price doubled within a day, rapidly pushing the company's market capitalization to around $2.7 billion. This kind of value would traditionally take years to decades to achieve, even for highly successful companies. The Netscape bonanza marked the indisputable beginning of the Internet era, and the floodgates were open to various online businesses.

Pets.com was one of the most emblematic Internet startups of the dot-com bubble. As an online store for pet supplies, the company attracted attention through clever marketing as an early adopter of new technology that offered something that a lot of people needed. Like a lot of other dot-com startups, Pets.com was able to garner massive investment during the bubble, but most of that capital went to marketing, including expensive Super Bowl advertising, instead of building a sustainable business model. The company would take nine months to go bankrupt after its initial public offering. All the hype in the world and support from Amazon.com couldn't save Pets.com from its demise.

Throughout the late 1990s, most of these companies directed all of their capital toward advertising, acquisitions, and, in many cases, luxuries like big offices and vacations. The hype carrying the entire fad was so strong that just adding ".com" to the name of a business was sometimes enough to attract investment. Companies went public without even offering a concrete product, riding exclusively on the promise of grand things to come in a digital future. Profitability, valuation, assets, and other traditional metrics were described as outdated and somehow inapplicable to the shiny new age of technology.

On March 10, 2000, the NASDAQ Composite reached 5,048.62, doubling its value in a single year and rising 529% since 1995. The fever couldn't last forever, though; it would be all downhill from there. The ensuing collapse was accelerated by the Federal Reserve's plans to tighten monetary policies and by well-informed insiders beginning to cash out their stocks. The announced recession in Japan on March 13 would hit tech-related stocks particularly hard, and the pressure to sell would quickly spiral out of control.

As investors started to bail, companies found their cash reserves drying up fast. The United States entered a recession by March of 2001, and by October of 2002, the NASDAQ was at 1,114.11 points, down 77.9% from the height of the dot-com bubble. The IT sector descended into chaos, with over 400,000 jobs being lost. A few of the more successful dot-com companies were able to pull through and went on to become the mega-corporations known across the world today. For the majority, the bubble was a cruel reminder that novel ideas and capitalist manias are no substitute for a sensible business model.

Recap Questions

- How did public perception and trust in the banking system evolve after each of these economic events?

_____

_____

_____

_____

- In what ways did government intervention, or lack thereof, contribute to or mitigate these financial crises?

_____

_____

_____

_____

- What patterns of speculative behavior can be observed across these three distinct periods?

_____

_____

_____

_____

Chapter 4: Cold War Catastrophes

The United States had episodic experiences with great power politics well before World War II, such as the clashes with Britain and Spain and America's forays into colonialism in the Philippines and elsewhere. However, in the aftermath of World War II, the United States arose as an undisputed superpower with far-reaching influence worldwide and strong geopolitical and military footholds in Europe, Asia, and beyond.

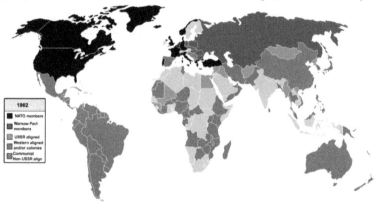

Cold War map.[12]

America's entry into this great game would not go unnoticed, nor would its claim to global supremacy go unchallenged. The worst war in human history had given birth to a major challenger in the form of the USSR and its allied bloc, and once the Soviets caught up to America's nuclear capabilities, the stakes were elevated to a level with no historical precedent. The inconceivable horrors of nuclear war presented a prospect that was just terrifying enough to prevent the two superpowers from going to war directly, but the rivalry played out in virtually all other arenas. The decades of the Cold War were ripe with close encounters, schemes, espionage affairs, proxy wars, and many scandalous blunders, quite a few of which belonged to the United States.

The Bay of Pigs Invasion

The Bay of Pigs Invasion was one of the most scandalous military blunders in American history. It was also one of the final steps toward the culmination of the deterioration in American-Cuban relations, which had declined rapidly following the revolution in 1959. The history of American relations with the island nation of Cuba is quite long and has never been all that positive, even before Fidel Castro's revolution. More often than not, the relations were an arrangement of complete American military, economic, and political dominance.

Following the decline of Spanish influence in the Americas, Cuba became an American protectorate in the late 19ᵗʰ century, only achieving formal independence in 1902. In practice, Cuban independence left a lot to be desired, with a consistent American military presence in Guantanamo, political control, and free reign for American companies to come in and conduct business as best suited them. Over time, this state of affairs led to a lot of discontent among the Cubans, many of whom had to contend with corruption and poverty in a country subordinate to a foreign power. In the 1950s, a lot of this anger would be directed toward the country's American-backed president, Fulgencio Batista.

The advent of communist ideas and the immense Soviet influence at the height of the Cold War opened the door to change, leading to the 1959 revolution led by Castro. The takeover of Cuba by a movement openly hostile to the United States expectedly caused outrage in Washington due to clear negative implications for America's national security. A Soviet-aligned country right in America's backyard, willing to engage in military cooperation with the Soviets and even allow troops and other assets onto the island, was unacceptable to the US. The infamous, almost apocalyptic Cuban Missile Crisis that came as a result of these tensions was a strong demonstration of just how seriously the US took this threat and how far they were willing to go to neutralize it.

The missile crisis, along with the subsequent complete collapse in American-Cuban relations, was the result of the Bay of Pigs incident.

Codenamed Operation Zapata after a coastal area in southern Cuba, the invasion was planned by the CIA in response to the revolution and the breakdown in communication with Cuba. It was meant to be a quick fix to a sudden problem aimed at neutralizing Castro and knocking the communists out of power. However, despite the checkered legacy of the revolution and the problems that plague Cuba to this day, Castro's movement was popular at the time. The CIA's plan was to recruit, train, and assemble around 1,400 anti-Castro Cubans who had been exiled in the purges following the communist takeover. Unfortunately for the CIA planners, this number of troops was nowhere near enough to face off with the revolutionaries, much less in a country that, by large, supported the new government.

Batista was essentially a dictator, which might have been tolerated better had there not been a range of other grievances that the Cubans had against him. Beyond the repressiveness and corruption of his regime, Batista was also a friend of American corporations, seen by many as foreign exploiters of the Cuban people. When Fidel Castro and his rebels emerged from the countryside and stormed downtown Havana on January 1, 1959, the old order collapsed quickly, often accompanied by celebrations in the streets.

During Batista's rule, American companies were privileged in Cuba's economy and owned around half of the lucrative sugar plantations in the country, in addition to mines, cattle farms, and other valuable real estate. Castro and his supporters wanted to end this and other arrangements with the US, ushering in an era of sovereignty, independence, and national revival within a communist framework. Most unnervingly, for Washington, this meant a drastic change in foreign policy and a suspension of military agreements and leases. As soon as Batista's government collapsed, the communists moved to eliminate American influence in the country. A wave of nationalizations across Cuba's industries began, accompanied by land reforms. Another major problem for the US was that Castro had ambitions to export the revolution as well, networking with other communists and left-wing leaders across Latin America.

The CIA's plan for the invasion was drawn up in early 1960 under Dwight D. Eisenhower, who gave the green light to the agency to make preparations. The army of 1,400 exiles was to be assembled mainly from the many Cubans living in Miami under the command of José Miró Cardona, who had once been associated with Castro. By early 1961, relations between the US and Cuba had been essentially abolished, and John F. Kennedy had assumed the presidency. Despite disagreements from some of his close advisors, JFK decided to stick with the CIA plan. The original design of the operation had glaring flaws from the get-go. Kennedy was also reluctant to overtly involve America in an invasion of Cuba because he was worried about retaliation from the Soviets. The CIA assured the president that US involvement could be minimal and would remain a secret. The weakness of the invasion force, according to the CIA, could be offset by an uprising against Castro from within Cuba, which would be triggered after the invasion began.

The Bay of Pigs was chosen due to its isolation and remoteness, which would allow an invasion force to make landfall covertly before moving deeper into the country. Part of the invasion force was loaded up into disguised B-26 bombers in Nicaragua and commenced the operation on April 15, 1961. An important early step in the plan was to destroy Cuba's small air force, which posed a considerable threat to the invasion force. Unbeknown to the Americans, however, Castro had already caught wind of their plan, which allowed him to hide the airplanes before the air strikes began.

The exile brigade likely believed they would receive further air support as the fighting commenced, but this would never come to fruition. As soon as the ill-fated operation began, Kennedy realized that the operation would be neither secret nor successful, but it was too late to call the thing off. On April 17, the main landings in the Bay of Pigs began, despite the complete failure of the opening stage of the operation. By this time, the Cubans had a radio station operating close to the beach, broadcasting the details of the engagement across Cuba as the disaster unfolded. Some of the landing vessels sank after striking coral reefs close to the bay, while paratroopers who were meant to provide crucial reinforcements missed their drop zones.

Caught between the shrinking prospects of success and the need to retain at least some deniability, Kennedy decided to forego further air support for the exiles. To the shock of the exiles and much frustration of the CIA, the president refused to escalate American military involvement, fearing a potential escalation into World War III. Stranded, disorganized, and seemingly abandoned, the exiles surrendered to Castro after less than a day, with over 100 killed in action.

John F. Kennedy.[13]

The invasion only strengthened Castro's revolution since it was an enormous propaganda victory for the communists. Within three days, Castro's image was solidified as that of a hero bravely fighting off the imperialists. More importantly, the disaster was a point of no return concerning American-Cuban relations, driving Cuba even further into the arms of the Soviets, which culminated in the 1962 missile crisis. The failure didn't stop the US from trying to overthrow Castro in the subsequent years, but it became clear that the CIA wasn't equipped to conduct and plan direct military operations. Efforts like Operation Mongoose became the new standard for CIA actions against Cuba, revolving mostly around sabotage, attempted assassinations, small-scale covert operations, and even terrorism. All attempts to overthrow Castro and his regime would ultimately fail.

The U-2 Incident

Apart from revolutions, counterrevolutions, coups, and other power struggles in countries caught between the superpowers, the Cold War's most famous feature was espionage. The two superpowers could not go to war directly as they both knew that the other side could destroy the other, all while constantly working to improve such capabilities. The Cold War was thus a period of profound paranoia on both sides and at every state level. Throughout this era, both the US and the Soviets would develop many creative, ingenious ways of keeping tabs on each other and uncovering as many military secrets as possible. Agents operating behind enemy lines might dominate spy movies, but in reality, some of the greatest investments were allocated to air assets, particularly spy aircraft.

The so-called U-2 incident in 1960 brought many revelations about such projects and the extent of espionage being carried out from the air. It also triggered a major international incident between the US and the USSR at a time when tensions were already reaching their peak. Aerial reconnaissance had already become a crucial aspect of intelligence gathering since the early days of the combat application of aircraft in the early 20ᵗʰ century. The Cold War brought technological advancements that propelled these capabilities to a whole new level. The Lockheed U-2 aircraft, colloquially called the Dragon Lady, was a highly classified project to improve such capabilities. The U-2 was instrumental in allowing the Americans to take a closer, more detailed look at Soviet nuclear capabilities.

The state-of-the-art airplane was first introduced around 1956 and is still in service today. Its incredibly high flight ceiling of around 80,000 feet (24,000 meters) made the U-2 difficult to detect and even harder to shoot down, making it one of the best air reconnaissance assets at the time. The altitude it consistently operates on necessitates special equipment to keep the pilot safe, including a partially pressurized space suit that ensures a stable and consistent oxygen supply. The suit is also necessary because the cabin is partially pressurized, which means that malfunctions resulting in a sudden depressurization would be dangerous without special equipment.

When the U-2 spy planes first started flying over the USSR in 1956, pilots were issued a poison needle that allowed them to escape capture via suicide if they ever crashed and were hunted by the enemy. Indeed, U-2 planes operated so deep inside enemy territory that sending a rescue team in the case of a crash was hardly ever a consideration. Later revelations showed that the Soviets had been aware of the U-2 program from early on. They could track the aircraft on their advanced radars but lacked the air or anti-air assets to reach targets at such altitudes. This changed in 1960 when the Soviets began fielding new surface-to-air missiles with increased capabilities.

When CIA pilot Francis Gary Powers took off on his mission on May 1, he was unaware of these new Soviet capabilities. The flight, which started out of Pakistan and was supposed to last around nine hours and end in Norway, ended above Sverdlovsk, today's Yekaterinburg in Russia. The first missile struck near Gary Powers' aircraft at a high altitude, causing the U-2 to descend. At a lower altitude, the spy plane was struck a second time and knocked out of the sky. Powers survived the impact and was able to eject, but he landed near a populated area and was quickly apprehended by Soviet troops.

The incident immediately triggered an international scandal, with both sides being careful not to show all of their cards. The Soviets went public with the fact that they had shot down a US spy plane, but no mention was made of the captured pilot. When the US government ran a cover story about a weather aircraft accidentally flying off course into Russia, Khrushchev then published a photograph of captured Gary Powers and indisputable evidence of the U-2's crash. The incident threw off plans for an important summit in Paris that was supposed to produce valuable agreements on nuclear de-escalation, which was supposed to take place on May 14.

Eisenhower tried to salvage the meeting by finally coming clean about the U-2 program before the summit, but the damage had already been done. The Soviets left the summit in protest, and agreements on disarmament collapsed soon thereafter. Coupled with the escalating situation in Cuba, the U-2 incident was another pivotal step in the lead-up to the Cuban Missile Crisis, one of the lowest and most dangerous points in the history of US-Soviet relations. Meanwhile, Powers was tried for espionage in the late summer of 1960 and sentenced to ten years in prison. He would ultimately serve less than two years of that sentence, being released after the Soviets exchanged him for one of their own captured spies, Rudolf Abel. Finalized in February of 1962, this was the first official spy swap between the US and Russia, a practice that in some way continues to this day.

The Iran-Contra Affair

The Iran-Contra Affair, the Iran-Contra Scandal, or simply Irangate, refers to the political fallout following the publication of one of the biggest flops of Ronald Reagan's time as president. The scandal revolved around clandestine, illegal arms trade and financing of dubious paramilitary movements. The affair occurred within the context of three important processes that were happening in the world and the United States in the early 1980s. Central to the whole affair was the brutal 1980s war between Iran and Iraq, which saw a number of foreign powers interfering politically and materially on both sides.

There was also the matter of an ongoing anti-communist uprising in Nicaragua by the so-called Contras, a movement supported by the United States. Thirdly, Reagan had won the 1980 presidential election, but his Republican party could not secure either the Senate or the House of Representatives. This balance of power made it difficult for the Reagan administration to bring many of its programs to fruition since the Democrat majority could block his initiatives.

An essential part of Reagan's program was the "Reagan Doctrine," which was a pledge to support virtually any movement in the world that was fighting communists. The overarching goal was to curb Soviet influence around the globe, and this doctrine would dominate the final decade of the Cold War. Nicaragua was one of the main stages of this clandestine confrontation between the superpowers in the early 1980s because of an ongoing insurgency by the right-wing Contras fighting against communist Sandinistas and their government.

Reagan's efforts to assist the Contras were stymied by the Democrat Boland Amendment in Congress, which put new constraints on the CIA and Department of Defense activities abroad. Many American politicians at the time didn't share Reagan's love for the Contras, particularly because they were heavily involved in major cocaine trafficking. The president, on the other hand, likened the Contras to America's Founding Fathers. National Security Advisor Robert McFarlane was thus tasked with finding covert ways of helping the Nicaraguan paramilitaries.

In the coinciding Iran-Iraq War (1980-1988), the US offered varying degrees of support to Saddam Hussein and his war effort due to America's conflict with Iran's Islamic government following the 1979 revolution. The US-Iran conflict back then, just like today, manifested itself in many different ways, one of which was through Iran-backed Hezbollah in Lebanon. In the lead-up to Irangate, Hezbollah was holding seven American hostages in Lebanon, and returning these hostages was another priority task for McFarlane. Since Iran had sent subtle requests to the US for weapons to fight the Iraqis, McFarlane saw an opportunity to marry his two main missions.

This was how the administration came to the idea of covertly selling weapons to Iran, in violation of its own trade embargo, and then using the untraced revenue to fund the

Saddam Hussein.[14]

Contras in Nicaragua. McFarlane hoped that granting Iran's request for weapons would motivate them to pressure Hezbollah – essentially an Iranian proxy – into releasing the hostages. An added bonus, McFarlane, though, would be an improvement in relations with Lebanon. Despite opposition from some members of the administration, Reagan approved the initiative.

By 1986, McFarlane's plan was showing certain results for the most part, but things came to a head when the Lebanese *Al-Shiraa* publication exposed the arms deal. The unveiled tangled web of proxies, clandestine activities, and illegalities truly epitomized Cold War politics. Reagan's first reaction was denial, but he would eventually acknowledge the clandestine deal with Iran and Hezbollah. The subsequent investigation revealed that around $30 million was made from the arms shipments, $18 million of which could not be tracked down. At that point, Lt. Colonel Oliver North decided to come clean, admitting that the money went to the Contras and that the operation was no secret to the administration.

The affair would remain a constant blot on Reagan's presidency for the rest of his term, with a number of highly publicized investigations accompanying the scandal. McFarlane, North, and 12 other people later faced charges. The president faced no charges as the Tower Commission found that his only fault was a lack of oversight over his subordinates, who ended up getting most of the blame. Oliver North was found guilty on several counts, but his sentence was generally light. He received two years of probation and was forced to pay fines totaling $20,000. In the years following the whole ordeal, North became a well-known conservative author and commentator.

Despite raising a few questions regarding the powers and overreach of the executive branch, the Iran-Contra Affair's impact on the domestic political landscape was relatively minor. Even though he broke America's own trade embargo on Iran and negotiated with Hezbollah, recognized by the US as a terrorist organization, he left the scandal and his term mostly unscathed. No significant reputational loss among his supporters occurred, and Reagan ended his two terms as a fairly popular president.

Recap Questions

- How did the Bay of Pigs invasion influence subsequent U.S. covert operations?

- In what ways did the U-2 Incident shape the course of the Cold War and diplomatic relations?

- How did the Iran-Contra Affair impact domestic views on executive branch overreach?

Chapter 5: Racial Tensions

One of the saddest truths in the history of American race relations is that the abolition of slavery was but a single step on a long journey toward equality, which in some ways continues to this day. Abolition was still one of the most important steps, of course, but as bloody as the Civil War was, it still left a lot of things unresolved. The fact that throughout the 20ᵗʰ century, the United States continued experiencing episodes of egregious racial violence is a major failure in itself. This is why talking about America's greatest historic blunders is impossible without discussing a few of the intense violent episodes between the races, all of which happened well after abolition.

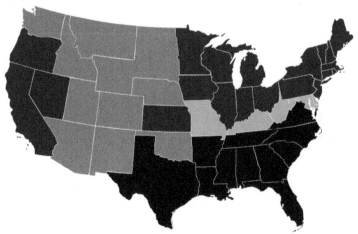

A map of the Civil War. The states in blue permitted slavery and the red states were Confederate states.[15]

The Tulsa Race Massacre

Apart from the carnage itself, one of the most unsettling aspects of the extreme outbreaks of racial violence in the 20ᵗʰ-century United States is that many of these incidents were buried and all but scrubbed from historical records for a long time. The 1920s were particularly violent not only due to rampant racism but also because economic competition exacerbated the problem. Yet despite the scale of the violence, the atrocities would be largely forgotten in the ensuing decades, sometimes taking upward of 70 years until proper investigations were carried out by the authorities. Not only did the perpetrators often get away with their crimes, but many of the victims were never identified and simply disappeared under the waves of indifferent history.

The 1921 Tulsa race massacre, also called the Tulsa race riot or the Black Wall Street massacre, was one of the worst examples of such violence. More precisely, the massacre befell the Greenwood neighborhood of Tulsa, Oklahoma, as armed mobs of White Tulsans razed entire blocks to the ground. Although it was one of the worst incidents of racial rioting that possibly led to hundreds of deaths, the massacre in Greenwood remained poorly understood and almost completely overlooked well into the 21ˢᵗ century.

By the early 1920s, Tulsa saw an incredible growth in population and economic prosperity, mostly owed to the oil industry. The city grew to over 100,000 people and was home to many entrepreneurs seeking their fortune in the growing markets. The population included around 10,000 Blacks. The usual racial segregation, quite common around that time, resulted in most of Tulsa's African-Americans concentrating in one particular neighborhood called Greenwood.

Despite significant crime rates and the overall weakness of law enforcement across the city, the community of Greenwood became a beacon of African-American entrepreneurship, especially in small businesses. One particular district of Greenwood was especially prominent for its thriving business community, which earned it the colloquial name of Black Wall Street. Greenwood was also known and praised for its self-sufficiency, as it was home to many Black professionals and educated folks who provided vital services. Greenwood had a chain of grocery stores, newspapers, doctors, dentists, lawyers, priests, and various entertainment centers like movie theaters, amounting to hundreds of businesses.

The Tulsa massacre happened at a time of resurgence in Ku Klux Klan's activities and an overall tense racial situation in the country. Numerous race riots had taken place in the years prior, notably during the Red Summer of 1919, when White mobs attacked Black residents in several cities in the Northeast and Midwest. Such incidents were further proliferated due to the frequent inaction and sometimes even complicity of local authorities. Lynching was also a tragically common occurrence. In the summer of 1921, the KKK was quite present in Oklahoma, with around 3,200 Tulsa residents belonging to the Klan.

The brutal sack of Greenwood came at the peak of a perfect storm that included racial and economic competition, disgruntled veterans in need of jobs, and a series of extremely violent incidents. It all began with a seemingly minor disturbance that the media would inflate to the point of explosion. On May 30, 1921, Dick Rowland went about his day and entered Tulsa's Drexel Building. All that is known to a certainty is that Rowland, a Black teenager, entered an elevator at some point, which was operated by a White girl by the name of Sarah Page. For unclear reasons, Sarah Page screamed at some point, and Rowland was seen fleeing the scene. Following a police report, Rowland was arrested the next day.

Even before the boy was in custody, local media began running wild with the story. The *Tulsa Tribune,* for example, ran the story on its front page, alleging without any evidence that Rowland had sexually assaulted Sarah. The baseless accusation spread through Tulsa's White community like wildfire, and the day wasn't even done before the first mob was formed. The enraged crowd swarmed the city courthouse and told the sheriff, Willard McCullough, to hand the boy over, presumably to be lynched. The sheriff refused the demand and instructed his deputies to barricade the building with the boy inside.

As rumors of a standoff and an attempted lynching spread among the Black community, a couple of dozen Black veterans of the Great War headed to the courthouse to help with its defense. The sheriff refused their offer of assistance even though the White mob was becoming increasingly aggressive. Another, larger group of Black residents returned to the courthouse as night fell, but they were vastly outnumbered by around 1,500 Whites. Shots were fired soon after that, and the Black residents withdrew to Greenwood, after which chaos began.

Armed White men, some of them deputized by the city, engaged in a string of violent acts against Black residents through the night of May 31. Things only got much worse as dawn broke on June 1, as rumors spread throughout the city that a Black rebellion was underway. Some even alleged that African-Americans from outside Tulsa were starting to come in to join the insurrection. By early morning hours, the White population of Tusla was engulfed in hysteria. Thousands of White Tulsans, many of them with firearms, stormed Greenwood, looting, burning, and pillaging everything in their path.

The rampaging mob wreaked havoc on 35 city blocks, destroying over 1,250 houses and looting hundreds of others. Many businesses and facilities were razed to the ground, including hospitals, libraries, schools, stores – and even churches! Some eyewitness testimonies later stated that the rioters even used several privately owned aircraft to circle above Greenwood and drop explosives and incendiary devices while also shooting at people from the air. Some of the men in the aircraft were allegedly law enforcement officers.

Responding firefighters were powerless to slow down the carnage since they were threatened and forced to leave. The governor eventually deployed the National Guard, but the rioters had already laid waste to Greenwood by that time. The first National Guard wave consisted of over a hundred troops, with martial law being declared before noon and more troops arriving later. The subsequent testimonies about the work of the National Guard were mixed. Troops helped put out the fires and even came under attack from the rioters at times, but a large portion of their engagement consisted of taking Black citizens into custody and disarming them. On June 2, around 6,000 people were in custody, mostly Black Tulsans.

After the carnage finally subsided, the police dropped all charges against Dick Rowland, concluding that, in all likelihood, no incident of a sexual nature had transpired in the Drexel Building. The investigation found that it was either a simple accidental stumble on Rowland's part or that he might have stepped on Sarah's foot, which could have startled the girl. Throughout the riots, the sheriff's office was able to protect Rowland in the courthouse, allowing him to leave Tulsa alive in the aftermath of the massacre.

Many other Black Tulsans would follow suit after the massacre, leaving Tulsa never to return. With around 10,000 African-Americans left homeless and no justice or compensation in sight, many residents felt that their only recourse was to move on. Still, many stayed and gradually rebuilt their lives, although they would have to carry their wounds in silence. In the end, the role of irresponsible yellow journalism was pivotal in the nightmare that befell Tulsa in 1921, but no media was willing to talk about the aftermath. Anywhere between 36 and 300 people were killed in the pogrom, yet the entire ordeal was swept under the rug with shocking ease.

The KKK is a group of hateful white supremacists.[16]

The victims had virtually no way of getting compensation for the damages, injuries, and deaths, but there was also the matter of fear. For a long time following the massacre, Tulsa became increasingly segregated, and the KKK only grew more powerful. Decades passed without any commemoration of the events, and coupled with an apparent suppression of archives by the police and state militia, the massacre was all but forgotten. Some interest in the Tulsa riot began in the 1970s, but 1996 marked the first year the massacre was commemorated in a church service, with a new memorial added at the Greenwood Cultural Center. Investigative efforts intensified in the late 1990s with an official government commission. Only in the 21 century have investigators begun uncovering unmarked graves, as the truth of the massacre began making its way into school textbooks.

The Rosewood Massacre

The Rosewood Massacre, which occurred just two years after the dreadful events in Tulsa, followed a similar pattern of escalation, violence, and subsequent historical obfuscation. In this case, the press didn't instigate the initial outbreak of violence, but they certainly added fuel to the fire once it began. The massacre in Rosewood was also a longer violent episode with more permanent consequences, lasting for days and resulting in the complete destruction and exodus of the town.

By the time of the massacre, the Floridian town of Rosewood had become an entirely Black settlement through a combination of segregation in the Jim Crow era and economic factors. The original settlement emerged in 1845, becoming home to a mixed population of Whites and Blacks. Following the Civil War and segregation years in Florida and much of the South, the races lived separately in Rosewood but still shared the town. The exodus of White residents began in the 1890s as the local industry involving cedar dwindled. Most of these families found a new home in Sumner, a town close to Rosewood. In the 1920s, only one White family remained, running a local general store in Rosewood.

Trouble began on January 1, 1923, in Sumner. Just like in Tulsa, everything started when a woman was heard screaming with no clear signs as to what exactly happened. A neighbor heard the screams of 22-year-old Fannie Taylor and rushed to see what was going on, only to find the young woman bruised and distraught. Unlike Tulsa's Sarah Page, Fannie Taylor didn't leave much to interpretation. She immediately alleged that she was assaulted by a Black man who broke into her home. The horrified neighbor promptly alerted the town's sheriff, Robert Elias Walker. Fannie went on to say that she was beaten but not raped.

The sheriff's department didn't have much to work with, but Fannie's husband, James, had all the information he needed. He immediately began assembling a mob for the hunt, not just in Sumner but also in nearby counties. A KKK rally was taking place in Gainesville at the same time, with around 500 Klan members volunteering for the search. Simultaneously, news broke that a Black fugitive, Jesse Hunter, had recently escaped somewhere in the area. The enraged residents and law enforcement assumed that Jesse was the likely culprit, and so they set out on their search. After they combed the nearby woods and found no Black man, the mob arrived at the conclusion that local Blacks must be hiding the fugitive.

The violence in Rosewood began with the kidnapping and beating of Aaron Carrier, who was taken from his home, tied to a car, and dragged to Sumner. At this early stage, the sheriff still tried to retain some semblance of order by taking the beaten and tortured man into protective custody and transferring him to safety in Gainesville. Unfortunately, the sheriff's complacency would only grow as the mobs got wilder. Blacksmith Sam Carter was the next victim, subjected to torture until giving a false confession that he was harboring Hunter. When he expectedly failed to show the fugitive whom he was supposedly hiding, the mob simply shot Carter and hung him from a tree.

A series of lynchings continued in the coming days, with many Blacks fleeing the violence and hiding in the home of Sarah Carrier, the aunt of Aaron. Sarah's home was the next target of mob violence as a mob descended upon the property on the night of January 4. Once again, the mob demanded the residents hand over Jesse Hunter. The non-existence of this fugitive anywhere close to the Carrier residence only enraged the lynch mob. A firefight ensued around the besieged house, killing Sarah, her son Sylvester, and two White attackers. As the mob forced their way into the home, the children who had taken refuge with Sarah fled into the woods.

Sadly, the first few days were merely the beginning of something much worse. This was also when newspapers started getting involved, spreading unsubstantiated numbers of victims and implying a widespread attack on Whites. Rumors about mobs of Black people with weapons rampaging around White areas were also spread, dramatically inflaming the situation. This attracted more White volunteers from the surrounding counties. As an ever-growing mob stormed Rosewood, the attackers burned churches, set fire to homes, and shot people as they fled. Many residents, along with their children, found refuge in the nearby swamplands, some of them hiding there for days.

All the while, some White families in nearby settlements provided shelter for the fleeing Rosewood residents. A famous philanthropic episode in the ordeal was that of William and John Bryce, two brothers who owned a train that they drove close to Rosewood to evacuate the women and children. Unfortunately, they generally didn't allow men on board, fearful that the mob would attack the train and kill everyone. John Wright, the owner of a general store in Rosewood, also distinguished himself by sheltering many residents, some of whom were later smuggled to the Bryce train. While Sheriff Walker's inaction was probably partly to blame for the massacre, some witnesses later stated that he did help victims get safely to Wright's house.

Throughout the peak of chaos, Governor Cary Hardee's offer to send the National Guard to quell the unrest was on the table, but the sheriff declined and argued that everything was under control. The rampage lasted until January 7, by which time much of the mob went home. On that day, some of the attackers went back to Rosewood to raze its last remnants to the ground, with only John Wright's home remaining intact. A subsequent investigation processed dozens of witnesses, most of whom were White, and the process ultimately produced no charges.

The official tally of casualties in the immediate aftermath listed a total of eight killed, six of them Black and two White. In all likelihood, the true death toll was much higher. The town was left unlivable, and the surviving residents never returned. The largely forgotten massacre only resurfaced in the 1980s owed to a few media investigations, notably the efforts of *St. Petersburg Times'* Gary Moore. When the public learned what had happened, the living survivors were encouraged to step forward and demand reparations. Florida eventually passed a bill that awarded $2 million to the plaintiffs. More importantly, the massacre was finally etched into history books and solidified in popular culture thanks to John Singleton's 1997 movie *Rosewood.*

The Watts Riots

The nature, cause, and methods of violence during the Watts Riots resulted in the event which also became known as the *Watts Rebellion.* It was a more recent incident, beginning on August 11, 1965, in LA's neighborhood of Watts. This mostly African-American neighborhood witnessed six days of extreme unrest that involved mob violence, weapons, widespread destruction, and 34 deaths. Over a thousand people were injured and around 3,500 arrested, as some 34,000 residents laid waste to the entire area, destroying around 1,000 buildings in the process. The total damages amounted to over $40 million, well over $300 million when adjusted for inflation. In many ways, the Watts Riots were emblematic of the heightened racial tensions at the peak of the civil rights movement and an eternal mistrust between law enforcement and the African-American community.

Burning buildings during the Watts riots.[17]

Much like the even worse LA riots of 1992, the 1965 chaos in Watts began with a traffic stop. It all started around 7 PM on August 11, an otherwise normal Wednesday evening. An officer of the California Highway Patrol pulled over two stepbrothers, Marquette and Ronald Frye, on suspicion that Marquette was drunk driving. The officer administered a field sobriety test, but Marquette failed it. Everything went wrong as the officer attempted to place him under arrest, leading first to a scuffle and then a rapidly escalating brawl involving an ever-growing crowd of backup cops and locals.

Even the mother of the two men, Rena, got involved when she stumbled upon what she thought was random abuse against her sons. After the Fryes were arrested with ample force, the massive altercation continued. Somewhere in the chaos, a cop was spat on by a woman whom they then tried to arrest. The crowd interpreted the woman to be pregnant, which escalated their rage beyond all control. Within 45 minutes of the routine traffic stop, all hell broke loose in Watts.

That night, the unrest evolved into what was essentially a race riot. A mob of locals attacked passing motorists at random, hurling bricks, rocks, bottles, and other objects. They also began targeting White drivers, pulling them from their vehicles and assaulting them. The Frye stepbrothers and their mother were released on bail the following morning, after which they joined a public meeting of local community leaders that convened in an attempt to appeal for calm. The police, church representatives, members of the NAACP, and many others participated. During this meeting, the underlying source of rage came to light as attendees began listing an endless array of grievances against the police and government officials. The crowd made references to a history of unfair treatment, at which point a young Black man rushed the stage and announced that the mob was preparing to march on White neighborhoods of LA.

After LAPD Chief William H. Parker refused to dispatch more Black cops and considered calling the National Guard, the rioters became even angrier. As the situation worsened, 14,000 National Guardsmen were deployed to stop the widespread looting and destruction. As rioters attacked firefighters and prevented them from putting out fires, unknown individuals started taking potshots at cops, reportedly with sniper rifles. Amid the chaos, Parker proclaimed that the mob consisted of "monkeys in a zoo" and made allegations that Muslims were to blame for the chaos. On the last day of the riot, police conducted a raid against a local mosque, which resulted in gunfire, mass arrests, and the destruction of the mosque after a fire broke out.

The sudden calamity, in some ways a race riot in reverse, shocked LA and the nation. Some of its aftermath was constructive, however, as it led to certain reforms that improved the community by addressing housing, employment, schooling, and healthcare inequalities. Community outreach by the police was also emphasized. The riot also motivated local Black communities to organize better and revise the ways in which they conduct activism. Unfortunately, the riot in Watts was just one in a string of similar incidents that struck numerous cities across the US between 1964 and 1965. The riot also motivated other attempts at decentralized uprisings, such as the deadly Detroit Riots two years later.

Recap Questions

- How did media portrayal and coverage play a role in shaping the narrative around these events?

_____

_____

_____

_____

- In what ways did these incidents influence subsequent civil rights movements and policies?

_____

_____

_____

_____

- What shared societal triggers can be identified across these three disparate events?

_____

_____

_____

_____

Chapter 6: Military Engagements

Apart from economic upheavals and ethno-racial tensions, another well-known feature of the darker side of American history has been warfare. Various figures about America's track record in regard to years of continuous peace have been thrown around for a long time. Some say that, since its founding, the United States has had 15 years of uninterrupted peace, while others say it was 17 years or some other approximation.

To say that the United States has been continuously at war for 90% of its history is, of course, an oversimplification of history, but the stereotype is certainly related to the truth. Major wars, small wars, limited foreign interventions, and conflicts by proxy; the United States was never a stranger to military confrontation. For a country that's been around for almost 250 years, that much warfare was always going to result in quite a few military blunders, some more consequential than others. Some of these wars have also been incredibly controversial and widely regarded as unjustified use of force, especially in recent history.

An image of US army men.[18]

The Vietnam War

Perhaps the highlight of America's troubles in the tumultuous years of the Cold War, the US commitment to Vietnam remains the greatest military blunder in American history. The disheartening ratio between blood invested and gains made in Vietnam is only overshadowed by the American Civil War, but that conflict at least led to a resolution that played a pivotal role in America's further development. The Vietnam War, on the other hand, brought nothing but tens of thousands of body bags, untold suffering for the Vietnamese people, debilitating divisions among Americans at home, generational trauma, and an unequivocal military defeat.

Following the hopeless attempts by France to retain its colonial hold over Indochina in the wake of World War II, the old European power called it quits in 1954. That year, the Geneva Conference resulted in the independence of a number of states in what was once French Indochina, with Vietnam itself divided into two countries. The principal victor of the First Indochina War against France was a Vietnamese national independence coalition commonly known as Viet Minh. In a way, it was a precursor to the famous Viet Cong movement, which was led by Ho Chi Minh and was based in the north of Vietnam.

Although Ho Chi Minh had once been more open to the West, even looking toward an alliance with the United States during the years of

Japanese imperialism in the region, things would change as the Cold War accelerated. America's alignment with France would disillusion many Vietnamese nationalists like Ho Chi Minh, who once considered America to be a potential constructive actor in the decolonization and expulsion of France. As the French foothold in the region collapsed, the Vietnamese liberation movement considered the job only halfway done, with their eyes looking hungrily toward the south. In the lead-up to the more famous Second Indochina War (1955-1975), which involved the US between 1965 and 1973, Ho Chi Minh's liberation movement would become communist in name. It's been somewhat debated how devoted Ho Chi Minh truly was to the ideas of Karl Marx and Lenin, but his public communist orientation secured essential assistance and support from the Eastern Bloc.

The other part of Vietnam that achieved independence in 1954, at least nominally, was the State of Vietnam, later known as South Vietnam. France initially retained a degree of influence over the nascent state, but as time went on, its role would be gradually taken over by the United States. For the United States, the prospect of a northern takeover across Vietnam meant the unification of Vietnam under a communist government hostile to American interests. At the time, the so-called domino theory was pervasive in the establishment of American foreign policy, manifested earlier in Korea. It revolved around the idea that any successful communist revolution would inevitably be exported, leading to a chain reaction in which states would fall under communist rule one by one.

This doctrine is widely criticized nowadays, but in the 1950s and 1960s, such a mentality was somewhat vindicated by the Cuban Revolution and similar events. Since stopping the spread of communism was one of the top items on Washington's agenda during the Cold War, getting involved more deeply in Vietnam must have seemed only natural. With France vacating the premises and North Vietnam firmly supported by great communist powers, it was only a matter of time before the North would try and realize its goals. This is how the US became involved in the seemingly irrelevant postcolonial affairs of a small country on the other side of the planet.

It began with material and political support for South Vietnam, but the US eventually became more directly involved through military advisors, intelligence agencies, and other more restrained methods. Following the controversial 1964 incident in the Gulf of Tonkin, legislators introduced a resolution that allowed the president to commit troops without a formal declaration of war. This was a significant boost to the power of the executive branch, and it allowed Lyndon Johnson to expand America's military presence in South Vietnam to around half a million troops by 1968.

The trouble with assisting South Vietnam was that it required much more than just safeguarding it from a North Vietnamese invasion. The countryside of South Vietnam was teeming with Viet Cong guerrillas and their sympathizers, all of whom worked toward Ho Chi Minh's dream of a united Vietnam free from all foreign control. As they crept through the jungles and stalked the alleyways of South Vietnamese cities, the VC refrained from no means toward their goal. Assassinations, bombings, executions, kidnappings, and even massacres were just some of the methods utilized. On the flip side, the VC – and anyone even remotely suspected of aiding them – were subject to the same treatment by the South Vietnamese government, often with American oversight. In these conditions, the ugliness of the Vietnam War was matched only by the speed with which its brutalities escalated.

The VC famously proved to be elusive, tough, clever, and ruthless as an enemy to American GIs in the country. They could strike virtually anywhere and at any time, inflicting terrible losses before disappearing into the countryside. The difficulty in identifying the VC and their sympathizers among the rural population was one of the main reasons why America's involvement in the war got so messy. Powerless to deal with these hit-and-run tactics, the US tried to fight the grueling guerilla war as best it could. Counter-guerrilla units were formed and sent deep into the jungle, highly effective on the individual level but barely making a dent in the grand scheme of things.

Mostly, the US resorted to endless bombing in both Vietnam and the neighboring Laos and Cambodia. In total, the US military dropped more than 7,000,000 tons of bombs across Indochina, compared to a total of 2,100,000 tons in both theaters during the entirety of World War II. There weren't that many rules of engagement preventing bombing raids against North Vietnam, although the doctrine varied somewhat during the war. In all, North Vietnam was bombed extensively, but the North Vietnamese Army was equipped not just with aircraft but also state-of-the-art air defense systems supplied by the Soviets. This made sorties over the North incredibly dangerous. By the end of the war, the US would lose around 10,000 aircraft of all types across the war zone.

Helicopters and UAVs contributed a lot to this staggering figure, but NVA SAM systems also wreaked havoc on fixed-wing aircraft.

Frustrated and demoralized troops, often at the end of their wits, would routinely inflict their vengeance on the populace. High-profile incidents such as the horrific My Lai Massacre drove the point home quite literally, causing outrage and rapidly growing disillusionment with the war in the American public. Perhaps the largest anti-war movement in American history eventually grew to a point where it could no longer be ignored. The stated initial goal of preventing the spread of communism was nowhere near enough to convince the people that tens of thousands of casualties and all the suffering in Vietnam were worth it.

Ultimately, public opinion was the decisive factor that brought down the whole house of cards. Throughout the 1960s and early 1970s, the war profoundly affected the polarization in the United States. Political, cultural, generational, and class divisions reached their all-time high, threatening the very fabric of American society. It was also a time rife with political violence and assassinations. Public opinion shaped the war, but the war exerted even more effect on the public. An entire generation of Americans was irreversibly changed by the Vietnam War, with some scars visible to this very day.

The war's conclusion came a couple of years after the US had already mostly disengaged from Vietnam. Under their red banner, the North Vietnamese triumphantly marched into Saigon on April 30, 1975, as the last remnants of American personnel and their local allies clung to helicopters in a chaotic, last-minute evacuation as the communists besieged the US embassy. Three decades of warfare had passed since the onset of the First Indochina War, and Ho Chi Minh's dream was finally realized, although the man had died six years prior.

Although Vietnam had now become unified and independent, it still wasn't over. The troubling situation in neighboring Cambodia had spiraled out of control, provoking a Vietnamese intervention against Pol Pot, all while China loomed ominously over Vietnam's northern frontier. War and Vietnamese occupation in Cambodia, border clashes with China, friction and sporadic violence lasted all the way until 1991 when the region finally descended into peace. While the loss of prestige and the psychological trauma of the war are still felt in America today, the deepest scars remain in Indochina. Unexploded ordnance, environmental devastation, and birth defects caused by chemicals like

Agent Orange are issues that Indochina still contends with. In the end, the fact that not a single American goal was achieved in spite of all this carnage, which included 58,281 American deaths, cements Vietnam as America's greatest military blunder to date.

The Korean War

One of the hardest things to explain about the Korean War is its colloquial name, which is the "Forgotten War." The epithet undoubtedly holds water since the Korean War is indeed rarely talked about in the United States, although it's difficult to ascertain why. It's certainly not for a lack of carnage during the war. Lasting just a bit over three years, the war was much shorter than the one in Vietnam, yet it killed millions, including an estimated two to three million civilians. It also featured some of the most destructive campaigns of aerial bombing in American military history.

A train attack during the Korean War.[19]

The Korean War was also an incredibly high-stakes conflict, bringing the world dangerously close to atomic warfare. In Korea, American and allied forces under the UN banner fought a direct ground war against Chinese troops, with China eventually committing up to three million total troops to the war. The great power confrontation notably took place in the air, which even drew in the Soviets, who sent unmarked aircraft with Russian pilots to fight directly against the US Air Force. This was also the first war in which jet fighters on two sides faced each other in air combat. Throughout the war, the US considered and threatened to deploy nuclear weapons on the battlefield. Especially notable was General Douglas MacArthur's contingency idea to attack both North Korea and China with atomic bombs, not just to destroy important targets but to create "radioactive fallout zones" as a method of area denial and supply disruption. Fortunately, such ideas never came to fruition.

Another reason the Korean War should not be forgotten is its enormous geopolitical and security ramifications. In many ways, the unresolved Korean conflict continues to profoundly affect the lives of people all across East Asia, especially now that North Korea wields a nuclear arsenal. The only logical explanation for the Korean War fading from American memory is that it occurred right between World War II and the Vietnam War, which completely overshadowed the events in the Korean Peninsula. Still, the US suffered close to 140,000 casualties in the war, including over 36,000 deaths, a horrendous amount by today's sensibilities.

Critics sometimes argue that the US has had a vested interest in sweeping the war under the rug due to its sheer brutality and massive civilian casualties. The same could be said about the Vietnam War, however, and that conflict has firmly entrenched itself deep into American national consciousness and culture. Nonetheless, the human cost of both these wars was comparable in terms of people killed, but the difference is that the Korean War lasted a fraction of the time.

Part of the casualties came from three years of heavy fighting accompanied by massive army movements as the frontline swung between the north and south. There was also no shortage of atrocities among the Koreans themselves, whether in reprisals by the communist North or anti-communist purges and political prison camps in the South. However, perhaps the most destructive and lethal factor in the war was the bombing, which the United States carried out extensively and on an enormous scale in both Koreas.

The total tonnage of bombs deployed on the Korean Peninsula was comparable to that of the entire Pacific War against Japan, a fate that Vietnam and its neighbors would also endure in the following decade. With around 635,000 tons of bombs dropped, the Korean Peninsula is listed as one of the most heavily bombed places in history. The tonnage was still far surpassed by South Vietnam and Laos, which received

4,000,000 and 2,000,000 tons, respectively, but North Korea ranks among the top five most bombed countries nonetheless.

It's also important to consider factors like territorial size, population, and timespan of the bombings to truly put Korea's destruction in perspective. Virtually no significant structure in North Korea remained standing by the end of the war, with huge swaths of the population living much of their lives underground. Simple villages, as per Douglas MacArthur, became legitimate military targets. Toward the end of the war in 1953, the US deliberately bombed a number of major dams, which caused flooding and widespread destruction of rice crops. A massive famine was likely prevented only by swift assistance from North Korea's communist allies, as rice was a critical, life-sustaining resource. A number of critics have described the targeting of civilians in Korea as war crimes, with historian Bruce Cumings going as far as calling it genocide.

It's also worth pointing out that over 32,000 tons of napalm was used in the bombings, a substantial amount that's often overshadowed by napalm's pop-culture association with Vietnam. In 1988, former general Curtis LeMay made an off-hand estimate that about 20% of the North Korean population (around 10 million at the time) was "killed off" in the three years of war "as direct casualties of war or from starvation and exposure." General LeMay himself was one of the masterminds behind the bombing campaigns in Korea and in the war against Japan years prior.

Also similar to the Vietnam War were the origins and initial triggers of the full-scale war. The conflicts are often compared due to their many parallels, although significant differences exist. The division of Korea between the communist-influenced north and a western-aligned south also happened in the wake of World War II. However, Vietnam had a long experience of Western colonialism to boot, unlike Korea, which was mostly familiar with Japanese imperialism primarily. When the Japanese were driven out of Korea, the US and USSR split Korea into two parts under their respective influences. It wasn't long until tensions flared up, and the two Koreas engaged in direct combat.

America's intervention began following North Korea's invasion of the South in 1950. The North Korean push was fast, ruthless, and highly effective, bringing the communist forces within a proverbial inch of capturing the entire peninsula. America and a number of other countries were deeply unsettled by the sudden dash to the south, with the US interpreting it as an unprovoked act of aggression encouraged by the Soviets. There has been some controversy around who fired the first shot and whether the attack was unprovoked, but there is no doubt that the Korean War began in earnest with the DPRK's southward push.

The US was fairly quick to respond, assembling a coalition of allied countries and even securing a UN Security Council mandate for the invasion force to push back the North Koreans. This gave the coalition a degree of legitimacy and is the reason why history often refers to the allied forces as "UN forces." In reality, the mandate was obtained at a time when the USSR was boycotting the UNSC. The boycott was a way of protest against the Western powers' refusal to acknowledge the new reality in mainland China, still insisting that the Republic of China, by then just the island of Taiwan, continue representing China at the UNSC. In practice, this meant that there was no opposition to the Western motion to intervene in Korea, even though the Soviets would have undoubtedly vetoed the proposal under normal circumstances.

With a number of UN states at their back, the South Koreans were immediately brought back into the fight. The coalition soon pushed the DPRK troops north and threatened to unify all of Korea under the southern, US-aligned government. As soon as the coalition crossed into North Korea, China responded in a shocking fashion by sending an expeditionary force to face the Americans and their allies. The hot war continued until July 27, 1953, when the situation was eventually stabilized along the 38th parallel. The formation of the Korean Demilitarized Zone along this line put a stop to major operations, but the war was never formally concluded.

Historiography records this war as a draw due to its inconclusive result, but a case can easily be made that it was a considerable blunder for the US. For that much destruction and death, the war accomplished very little. The US failed to resolve the Korean issue both in practice and on paper. Since no formal treaty was ever signed, the conflict has remained a constant source of tension that has erupted into lethal violence on many occasions since 1953.

A minor victory resides in the fact that today's South Korea is a much more prosperous country than its northern cousins, who live in what is widely regarded as the most repressive system of government on the planet. In military terms, however, North Korea has only grown stronger and has essentially assured its security by obtaining nuclear weapons. In terms of security and political goals, the war changed very little for the Koreans on both sides of the DMZ.

China's results, despite heavy casualties, are perhaps the only outcome that could be interpreted as a success. For the Chinese, the intervention was simply about driving the Americans away from their border and keeping them as far away as possible. North Korea fulfills this purpose very effectively as a buffer zone that's not going anywhere any time soon. It can also be argued that the Chinese intervention in Korea made the US reluctant to invade North Vietnam during the conflict in Indochina, opting for a more restrained approach that only focused on preserving South Vietnam as a state instead of conquering the north, which borders China. This reluctance was widely criticized by many supporters of the Vietnam War, and the constraints that were in place are still cited as one of the reasons the US lost the war in Vietnam.

The Iraq War's WMD Controversy

In the post-Cold War world, the United States emerged as the undisputed global superpower with a military, political, or economic foothold in almost all corners of the world. One of the first major confrontations that the US would have with another country in this new world began before the USSR even officially collapsed, and that was Iraq. While he had previously been periodically friendly with the US government, especially during his war against Iran in the 1980s, Saddam Hussein became increasingly problematic for the US around 1990.

The US Air Force landing over the Kuwaiti oil fires set by the Iraqi army.[20]

In August of that year, Iraq invaded and annexed neighboring Kuwait, which was the final straw for the US and many other countries, especially in the region. Thus began the first Gulf War, which resulted in one of the broadest and most diverse international coalitions ever assembled, all agreeing that Saddam must leave Kuwait. The 1991 Operation Desert Storm made short work of that goal, but the liberation of Kuwait was just the opening chapter to a much longer, bloodier story. More than a decade of excruciating sanctions and occasional bombing campaigns against Saddam's Iraq ensued, culminating in the events of 2003.

One of the key goals of the prolonged diplomatic and military standoff between the US and Iraq between 1991 and 2003 was the liquidation of Iraq's weapons of mass destruction. These WMDs mostly included biological and especially chemical weapons, which Saddam not only had but also demonstrated against his enemies more than once. Iranian troops and civilians, as well as Kurds within Iraq itself, were notable victims of multiple gas attacks in the 1980s. At one point, Iraq also likely had an early-stage nuclear program, which ultimately didn't go anywhere.

When the US began pushing for an invasion and the final overthrow of Saddam in the wake of 9/11, two main arguments were made in favor of the campaign. First and foremost were the allegations that the US constantly leveled against Iraq regarding its purported weapons program. US officials argued that despite UN inspections and in violation of UNSC resolutions, Iraq still maintained its stockpile of WMDs while also hinting at Iraq's alleged attempts at going nuclear. The second, equally unsubstantiated allegation was that Saddam had ties to al-Qaeda and was implicated in the 9/11 attacks. With both of the allegations, the official narrative was that Iraq presented a threat to American national security and the world.

In time, all of these allegations, including Secretary of State Colin Powell's infamous address to the UN General Assembly, have turned out demonstrably false. The Iraq War was ultimately a military blunder in many ways, but its instigation featured an element of deception that heavily impacted American credibility at home and abroad. In the years after the war, US officials have danced around the issue as much as possible, but when addressing it, the politicians would usually blame faulty intelligence. This gives the false pretenses an aura of negligence instead of malice, but the disastrous results of the war are difficult to argue with.

Despite hundreds of thousands of excess deaths from causes related to the war and untold billions invested into the war, no WMDs were ever found. Staunch critics have described the war as a deliberate war of aggression, with various factors cited as possible motives for the attack. The most popular, albeit shaky, theories revolve around Iraq's vast oil reserves. Others have suggested that the decisive factor was the influence of lobby groups from the private sector and America's foreign allies in the Middle East, who had a vested interest in overthrowing Saddam's admittedly vile regime.

Whatever the truth of the matter was, the war had far-reaching consequences that are still being studied and felt to this day. The invasion came at a time when the US was trying to assert itself as a global leader in a completely new world. It can be argued that the war severely damaged these attempts as it was carried out not just without a UN mandate but even without the approval of some of America's close European allies. Germany and France were vocally opposed to the war, which caused a degree of alienation for the Bush administration. Traditional Middle Eastern allies like Saudi Arabia were also deeply disturbed by the attack. The Saudi kingdom was one of the key American allies in 1991, providing spirited assistance and support for the effort to knock the Iraqis out of Kuwait. In 2003, however, the situation couldn't be more different.

Apart from America's loss of credibility and prestige, the war also wreaked havoc on the security situation in the Middle East, with effects felt far beyond. Iraq nowadays is on the verge of becoming a failed state and has experienced many episodes of horrendous sectarian violence and terrorism since Saddam fell. These problems have routinely spilled over across the region, destabilizing numerous countries and providing a suitable climate for the emergence of some of the worst excesses of terrorism the world has ever seen, including the Islamic State.

In strategic terms, purely through the lens of American geopolitical interests, the war has also been a failure. Iran, which is perhaps the primary adversary of the US and Israel in the Middle East, exerts more control over Iraq now than ever before. Widespread controversy and criticism completely envelop the Iraq war to this day, both at home and abroad, with the American public in recent years coming close to a consensus that the war was an unnecessary disaster.

The public opinion has evolved a long way since 2003. Even though there was a considerable anti-war movement in the early years of the invasion and occupation, the war retained a level of popularity that rode the wave of post-9/11 sentiments. In later years, however, the war has proven to have been one of the least popular conflicts America ever fought. It had a profoundly negative effect on the perceptions of American interventionism, with significant repercussions for subsequent foreign policies. The PR disaster was even worse internationally and has likely reduced America's ability to wield its military capabilities in international politics without significant criticism and pushback.

Recap Questions

- How did domestic public opinion shape, and get shaped by, the progression of these wars?

_____

_____

_____

_____

- What were the long-term consequences for the countries that were intervened in, both politically and societally?

_____

_____

_____

_____

- How did these military engagements influence subsequent U.S. foreign policy decisions?

_____

_____

_____

_____

Chapter 7: Big Brands, Big Blunders

For a very long time, one of the defining characteristics of American life has been innovation. Widely encouraged and heavily rewarded on multiple occasions, innovation quickly became one of the key driving forces behind America's economic growth and technological advancement. In fact, the emphasis on innovation in America, especially in business, has been so strong that it has led to a number of missteps and mistakes. In time, innovation has become something that consumers have come to expect from American companies, making the incentive to innovate powerful. At times, that incentive was so strong that it overpowered certain brands, leading to situations where innovation became the end instead of the means.

Coca-Cola is one of the many American brands that received backlash for their lack of market research.[21]

While it's a powerful tool in pursuing a goal, innovation for its own sake can result in misguided decisions. Incredibly unpopular changes to classic recipes like Coca-Cola, for instance, have proved that the consumer's hunger for novelty has its limits. Creative new solutions are appreciated, but so are classics, and some American brands have learned the value of balance between the two the hard way. Other seemingly innovative products have failed for different reasons, but all major blunders by big American brands have demonstrated the importance of market research.

The Edsel

Named after Henry Ford's son Edsel, the Edsel division was supposed to be Ford's new premier brand. Ford went all-in on this ambitious venture, sparing no expense on the project and especially its marketing. The development, manufacture, and marketing would end up costing the company $250 million in 1958 dollars, amounting to a whopping equivalent of around $2.5 billion in 2023 USD. The expectations for the new brand were at the highest level imaginable, not just for Ford but also for the public due to its overhyped marketing. Instead, the Edsel endeavor would become an emblematic flop and a cautionary tale for similarly ambitious business ventures in the decades since.

Ford's Edsel made its debut in 1957, a car born of ten years of development, planning, and high hopes. To make matters worse, it had been a long time since Ford had released a brand-new model, so a lot was riding on this launch. The Edsel offered 18 models to ensure the furthest possible market reach for the new brand. However, the massive investments that were made necessitated high goals in terms of sales. In fact, the Edsel would have to outperform all other 1957 cars by a significant margin if it were to become economically viable.

Following the launch in early September of 1957, the initial spike in interest would begin to subside relatively quickly. The 1958 Ford Edsel, specifically, was supposed to be developed based on polling data. For years leading up to the launch, Ford ran polls to figure out what the American people wanted from a car, intending to tailor their new model to the overarching desires deduced from the polls. This led to a lot of confidence in the company that the product could hardly fail. After all, the car was essentially built on driver input; at least, that was the story. In reality, Ford didn't really act on much of what was expressed in the polls. During the car's development, the vision gradually strayed from the research data as input from high-level executives slowly took over.

The vision also lost direction as time passed, with designers trying to make the car a jack of all trades, going in too many directions simultaneously. The 18 variants at launch were a testament to the diluted vision for the car, making the Edsel an automotive version of big tent politics. In an attempt to please everyone, the car ended up disappointing most people. Stranger yet was the apparently endless confidence that company executives had in the product, which can be inferred from the relentless marketing campaign before launch. Even the creation of the Edsel division was, in a way, part of the marketing campaign. The car was teased for about a year before it hit the market, referenced as the mysterious "E-Car," with connotations of futurism. Ford used its massive influence and clout to convince dealerships to order cars before they even finished development.

Ultimately, the Edsel launched as an overly expensive gas-guzzler with questionable aesthetics to boot. It was ravaged in the press, with a torrent of negative reviews doing irreversible damage to the nascent brand. Ford tried to redesign the Edsel in 1959, but even though the car was better, the brand was tainted. By 1960, the entire division was defunct, losing Ford some $350 million. Ford's reaction to the massive flop was also peculiar, demonstrating a lack of learning.

For instance, Edsel's marketing manager, J.C. Doyle, implied that the failure was the public's fault for being "fickle." In *Business Adventures* by John Brooks, Doyle was quoted as saying that the Edsel was the natural result of the hitherto purchasing habits of American drivers. As far

A 1958 Edsel Skyliner.[22]

as he was concerned, the industry had provided through Edsel exactly what the American public wanted, leaving him confused as to how it all went wrong. Instead, the Edsel has provided a case study of what not to do when developing and launching a new product.

Coca-Cola's Audacious Recipe Change

Even though it merely produces soft drinks and various refreshing beverages, the Coca-Cola Company has become one of the most domineering corporations on the planet. Part of this success has been owed to Coca-Cola's astronomical marketing budget, which has produced consistently successful advertising campaigns that have been so effective and for such a long time that it's practically a phenomenon. In recent years, the approximate annual advertising expenses for Coca-Cola have averaged around $4 billion across the world. The brand has made its way into every nook and cranny of the consumer markets and popular cultures in virtually every corner of the globe.

Despite all of this unprecedented success, Coca-Cola has been no stranger to major marketing flops. The most epic of such failures was undoubtedly the company's so-called New Coke in 1985, which was an attempt to reimagine a soda that the entire world had become accustomed to for many decades. Somehow overlooking the immense risk inherent to such a bold move, the Coca-Cola Company went ahead with the new recipe and encountered such an epic firestorm of backlash that they never tried anything similar again. In fact, Coca-Cola recorded over 40,000 complaints via letters and phone calls condemning the New Coke just a few months after its launch.

Coca-Cola's sudden attempt to fix what wasn't broken was so bizarre, unnecessary, and seemingly illogical that the controversy produced a number of conspiracy theories. Finding it hard to believe that such an enormous corporation would ruin its most important product for no apparent reason, people came up with theories suggesting it might have been a ploy to boost sales. A particularly popular theory argued that the formula was changed with the expectation that it would lead to a backlash. Then, after the return of the classic, sales would explode. Other popular speculations theorized that Coca-Cola created the controversy in order to cover up other, more subtle changes to its recipe. Some of these alleged changes included changing to cheaper sweeteners and eliminating the last remnants of coca from the recipe.

Conspiracy theories aside, the flop could have indeed been a textbook example of inadequate market research and miscalculation, showing that even the most powerful corporations are far from infallible. One suggested factor behind Coca-Cola's disastrous decision has been fear or paranoia over losing market share to Pepsi. Pepsi saw significant market expansion in the 1970s and early 1980s, partly due to clever and confident marketing. The so-called Pepsi Challenge, for instance, was a campaign that produced great results and caused unease at Coca-Cola.

The challenge involved a series of publicized taste tests where participants would go in blind to try both Coke and Pepsi and decide which tasted better. Quite a few people ended up preferring Pepsi, and aggressive marketing did the rest. The true shock came for Coca-Cola when it ran the same tests internally and found the same results. Throughout all this competition, Coca-Cola remained the most popular soda in the world, but the mere prospect of losing more market share to Pepsi was terrifying enough for the company to take drastic steps.

While working on the development of Diet Coke in the early 1980s, the company ran a number of taste tests among employees. One of those tests showed that a sweeter version of the drink fared better than both Pepsi and the old-fashioned Coke. This was how the idea for New Coke was born, and the recipe was unveiled to the world on April 23, 1985. The sudden change, coupled with negative press coverage, made New Coke dead on arrival. Some members of the press went as far as to describe New Coke as more like Pepsi, which would have been the final nail in the coffin. The price of Coca-Cola shares soon began to decline while those of Pepsi and other competitors grew. Pepsi showed no mercy, rubbing the salt into Coca-Cola's wound with massive newspaper advertisements that declared victory, saying that Coca-Cola had "blinked" after "87 years of going at it eyeball to eyeball."

Thousands of calls from disgruntled consumers buzzed Coca-Cola's offices every day. Some of the more extreme loyalists of the old recipe even staged protests, during which they demonstratively spilled New Coke into sewers and storm drains. The problem with Coca-Cola's market research wasn't that they didn't conduct it. Rather, the research they did was inadequate and failed to ask key questions. When the company made the decision to launch New Coke, they conducted close to 200,000 blind tests in North America.

The tests showed a good response to the new formula, but the company never asked the participants how they would feel if the new mix ended up replacing the classic. The emotional attachment that many consumers had developed for the old drink was something that the company completely failed to factor into their calculations. It's doubtful if such a thought even occurred to them, yet what Coca-Cola ultimately learned was that it had underestimated the loyalty of its own customers. Classic Coke was reinstated 79 days after the fiasco, accompanied by a public apology, massive media coverage, and an eventual spike in sales.

While New Coke was a massive flop, it was also a learning opportunity for Coca-Cola and other brands that paid attention. The strength of consumer loyalty and attachment to well-established brands was on full display. In the case of New Coke, that loyalty reminded Coca-Cola of its existence with a painful slap to the face, but the valuable lesson remained, ready to be harnessed in many marketing campaigns by countless companies to this day.

The Betamax Misstep

Sometimes called just Beta due to its logo, Betamax was a promising solution by Sony in an era when consumer-grade video recording began to proliferate. Betamax is most famous for being Sony's dog in the fight during the so-called videotape format war in the 1970s and 1980s. The intense rivalry between Betamax and Video Home System (VHS) saw two incompatible analog formats duke it out for dominion over an emerging market with a seemingly limitless promise of growth.

In this era of analog videotaping technology, magnetic tape was standard, with various companies offering their best attempts at making video cassette recorders (VCRs) as accessible and efficient as possible for regular consumers. Betamax and VHS emerged as the preeminent competitors, each providing some advantages over the other. For instance, Betamax tapes came in smaller cassettes that were more compact and offered better image quality. However, VHS tapes were longer, which ultimately proved to be the decisive factor.

Although VHS became absolutely dominant in time, it didn't completely knock out Betamax from the market, perhaps due to the latter's niche advantages. Recorders based on Betamax were manufactured and marketed well into 2002, at which point Sony finally discontinued them after 27 years. Since a number of Betamax recorders were still in circulation, blank Betamax cassettes kept being sold until 2016. Despite its overall failure among regular consumers, Betamax managed to find its niche among professional broadcasters, where it remained for quite a long time after VHS had already conquered households across the world.

Betamax had an early lead when it was released in 1975, quickly conquering the entire market, but VHS was quick to follow when JVC launched it in 1976. Already by 1980, VHS had expanded to around 60% of the home video market in North America. Sony's initial plan was to present its solution as having no alternative, hoping to dictate the standards of the industry by offering Betamax to JVC. However, JVC had its own development technology and felt it could do better if it launched its own product. Other companies would later follow JVC's example, destroying Sony's hopes that manufacturers would just adopt their technology while Sony reaped the profits.

The Betamax logo.[23]

When VHS hit the market, it was lighter and cheaper, and the compromise in sound and video quality was widely regarded as acceptable for the price difference. Professionals and studios might have cared about marginally better quality, but the average consumer who simply wanted to film birthdays and camping trips wasn't impressed enough to pay a higher price. Apart from being cheaper and offering a lot of the same functionalities with only a slight reduction in quality, VHS allowed for longer tapes. For many consumers, this was the main selling point.

Ultimately, JVC demonstrated a better understanding of what the average consumer wanted. Within a decade, the market share of Betamax dropped below 10%, leaving VHS as the undisputed king of home video. Sony tried to fight for years, introducing significant technological improvements like hi-fi audio, improved bandwidth, and a noticeable increase in video quality. While these improvements certainly piqued the interest of some enthusiasts, all they really did was ensure the price remained noticeably higher than that of VHS. Meanwhile, JVC worked on similar improvements as well, ensuring it maintained a steady hold over an ever-growing share of the market. In some ways, the video format war was a clash between the supposedly superior and the obviously affordable. The affordable turned out to be what the consumer truly wanted.

Recap Questions

- How did each company respond to the backlash or market rejection of their product?

\
\
\
\

- In what ways can these business missteps be viewed as both failures and learning opportunities?

\
\
\
\

- How have these historic corporate blunders influenced modern product development and marketing strategies?

\
\
\
\

Chapter 8: Sky-High Disasters

Some of the most important areas in which American innovation has spectacularly blossomed have traditionally been air travel and space exploration. The first airplane flew in North Carolina in 1903, following the successful development and testing by the legendary Wright brothers. During the space race, the Soviets had an early lead on a number of frontiers, but the incredible innovations by brilliant minds of science allowed America to catch up and eventually beat the Soviets to the moon.

Wright's first flight was in 1903, in North Carolina.[24]

Unfortunately, such epic endeavors rarely come without a cost. The towering ambitions of pioneers in the realms of air and space were tragically humbled on a number of occasions, but progress always found its way in the end. While pushing technological boundaries incurred a human cost, the indomitable spirit of exploration has consistently triumphed over setbacks, especially in the United States.

The Challenger Disaster

On January 28, 1986, the entire American public was given a first-hand look at the terrible price that space exploration can impose. It was a rare instance of an awful disaster that was broadcast live with millions of spectators tuning in through their TV sets. Among the seven crewmembers was Christa McAuliffe, a New Hampshire teacher who was supposed to become famous by being the first civilian to travel into space. Unfortunately, she and the rest of the crew would stay in memory as victims of one of the worst days of NASA's entire space shuttle program. Because McAuliffe was a teacher, the shuttle launch was watched by many American schoolchildren as well, making the whole ordeal even more unsettling.

January 28 wasn't the *Challenger* shuttle's first rodeo. The spacecraft had embarked upon nine missions prior to its dreadful end. The space shuttle program began in 1976, arising from the need to construct a reusable spacecraft that could conduct missions in space and then return safely to Earth to be used again. The program saw its first successful launch five years after it began, sending the space shuttle *Columbia* into orbit. *Challenger* was the second space shuttle in the program, conducting its maiden voyage on April 4, 1983.

The tragic flight was initially set for January 22, 1986, and was crewed by seven people. Christa McAuliffe was 37 years old at the time, having been picked by NASA for the Teacher in Space Program. Christa was a high school teacher and thus didn't have the usual credentials that astronauts are known for. The idea behind the program was to afford an opportunity for a regular American civilian to go into space, which required months of preparation and training.

After a short delay due to weather and technicalities, the mission was set to launch from the Kennedy Space Center in Florida on January 28. It was a cold morning, which was an easily identifiable potential problem for a shuttle launch. NASA's engineers knew as much, and they had no doubt that launching in such conditions was problematic. *Challenger's* O-rings, which were important components functioning as seals for the joints on the rocket boosters, were known not to fare very well in cold weather. The engineers told as much to their superiors, but their concerns were disregarded, and the mission was green-lit.

Liftoff was initiated at exactly 11:39 AM, watched breathlessly by hundreds of on-site spectators and millions at home glued to their TV sets. Just 73 seconds into the launch, *Challenger* exploded in a ball of fire and smoke as it was ripped to pieces as the families of the crew and a shocked nation watched in horror. Broken parts of the shuttle rained down into the ocean as every spectator realized that nobody could have survived such a fiery catastrophe. Indeed, everyone on board was surely dead instantly, and the fate of the entire space shuttle program was immediately put into question.

In the immediate aftermath, President Reagan organized an investigative commission to analyze the disaster and come up with measures to prevent its recurrence. Headed by William Rogers, the commission included experts such as Neil Armstrong and Chuck Yeager, a prolific test pilot. The Rogers Commission quickly found that, just as the engineers had warned, the O-ring seals failed as they became brittle at low temperatures. When the seals broke, fire from the solid rocket booster made its way to the external fuel tank, which suffered damage that led to the catastrophic explosion in flight. This glaring design flaw was the fault of the manufacturing company, Morton Thiokol, but the flaw was known. As such, NASA's upper management was also complicit in the tragedy.

The tragedy set back the entire space program, resulting in a suspension of manned space flights for over two years. The space shuttles were subjected to overhauls and redesigns, with flights resuming in September of 1988. That year, NASA successfully launched *Discovery, and the program ran smoothly for years to come, restoring much of the public's* trust in the space shuttle. Unfortunately, disaster struck yet again on February 1, 2003, when *Columbia* broke apart while reentering the atmosphere, once again killing all seven of the crewmembers. Another attempt to revive the space shuttle program was made in 2005, with flights continuing for a few more years until it was finally discontinued in 2011.

The Hindenburg Disaster

The massive airship *Hindenburg* was a true leviathan that loomed with dominance over any town or city she would visit. While her historic demise occurred in the US and can thus be categorized among American air disasters, the *Hindenburg* was not an American airship. In fact, she was the pride of the Third Reich, representing the latest and most luxurious trends in German airship engineering. In many ways, the *Hindenburg* was to air travel what the *Titanic* was to ocean travel.

The Hindenburg disaster.[25]

The LZ 129 *Hindenburg* was an enormous zeppelin, also known as a *dirigible*, which was constructed between 1931 and 1936 and launched just a year before its demise. In the interwar period, zeppelins were seen as a safe, fast, and comfortable mode of transportation, especially on cross-Atlantic journeys. The *Hindenburg* was a powerful giant, able to cross the Atlantic in half the time of the fastest ocean liners at the time. By the 1930s, airplanes were becoming more and more prolific, but many people still believed that airships were the true future of air travel. One of the main reasons for this was the comfort they allowed, which is impossible on airplanes.

Travelers in those days, especially wealthier ones, expected to enjoy amenities, space, and various luxuries when traveling by air, all of the things they had become accustomed to on ocean liners. The *Hindenburg* and other similar airships provided just that. Airline zeppelins had a much smaller passenger capacity than ships or today's commercial airliners, but being economical was perhaps not a major priority. Spacious personal quarters, a restaurant, and a piano-equipped lounging area were only some of the perks of crossing the ocean aboard the *Hindenburg*. The airship was operated by the German DZR airline, offering its clients an experience akin to a sky hotel.

By the time the *Hindenburg* crashed and burned, zeppelin air travel had a tradition of some 30 years with a good safety record. Because of the comforts they provided, the reduced travel time, and thousands of successful flights over the decades, there was no reason in the interwar period to think dirigibles would become unpopular anytime soon, especially at long distances. The 1937 disaster would deal a devastating blow to such notions, contributing to the rapid decline in the popularity of airships and the gradual rise of passenger airplanes.

This dramatic shift in public perception also serves as an early example of the power of visual media. The pictures and videos taken and widely publicized inspired shock and completely overshadowed the otherwise solid safety record that airships had. The footage of the floating leviathan's horrendous immolation is certainly unsettling, but it's doubtful that news of a single airship accident could have done the same amount of damage to the aircraft's reputation without the accompanying video.

Nonetheless, the disaster itself was objectively shocking and also deadly, killing a total of 36 people, including crewmembers, passengers, and one bystander on the ground. The *Hindenburg* burned down on May 6, 1937, while docked in Manchester Township, New Jersey. Despite her imposing size and impressive construction, the ship's major flaw and weakness was the lifting gas, in this case hydrogen, which was 7 million cubic feet worth. The massive aerostat was constructed with compartments that were meant to prevent a rapid spread of fire in case of an accident, but nothing went right on that day. Hydrogen was a highly flammable gas and, according to some, an accident waiting to happen. While it was cheaper, abundant, and offered better lift, hydrogen was well understood to be a fire hazard. The ideal choice was helium, but this is a rare, expensive gas that was subject to an American export ban at the time when the *Hindenburg* was being built.

The cause of the spark that ignited the spectacularly horrifying fire of *Hindenburg* has never been fully ascertained. As it attempted to make a landing, the airship was beset by difficult weather and a strange slacking of its tail section. At some point, a major gas leak erupted and was ignited by a spontaneous static discharge or an atmospheric spark. The massive and rapid inferno quickly engulfed a huge section of the aerostat before causing a massive explosion, as clearly depicted in the numerous photographs and videos of the incident. To this day, the material stands as a symbol of how an entire mode of transport went up in flames that day, both physically and in the public's perception. Zeppelins are still used to this day, but the industry would never fully recover from this German-American disaster.

The Apollo 1 Tragedy

Apollo 1 was meant to be the first manned launch of the legendary Apollo program, born of JFK's pledge to send a man to the Moon and return him safely to Earth. The mission was originally designated AS-204, but its tragic outcome motivated the widows of the departed astronauts to request its renaming to Apollo 1. The name Apollo was meant to be used for flights, which AS-204 never became since it catastrophically failed during a launch rehearsal on the ground.

The Apollo 1 Crew.[26]

Reserving the name Apollo 1 meant that the astronauts were at least symbolically given the long-awaited flight that they never got to make. This was a way to honor the sacrifices of the three astronauts who perished on this pivotal step toward making crewed missions to the Earth's natural satellite a reality. The three-man crew would eventually all posthumously receive the Congressional Space Medal of Honor as well. The crew included Virgil "Gus" Grissom, Ed White, and the least experienced among them, young Roger Chaffee.

The main phase of the mission launch was scheduled for February 21, 1967, with a period of intense testing preceding it. By that time, JFK's Apollo program wasn't going as smoothly as intended. Spacecraft designs were running late, throwing the whole program off schedule and pushing the first manned mission back. Many of the tests that were run on the spacecraft ended in failure, too, raising many concerns, not least of which were those by the astronauts themselves. All three astronauts were very outspoken about their misgivings at NASA and in public. They even made a photograph in jest, which showed them all praying while sitting around a small-scale model of their spacecraft.

In the early days of the Apollo program, nobody had any illusions as to the danger of the missions. This is why astronauts could psychologically tackle the threat of death in an almost comical spirit. The high goal of landing a man on the Moon was simply so overwhelmingly empowering that it overshadowed all fear. There was also a degree of hubris to the whole endeavor, stemming from the confidence that NASA had acquired from its numerous successful manned launches in the years leading up to Apollo 1. As flight director Gene Kranz put it in the book *Failure Is Not an Option,* "success had become almost routine."

Nonetheless, the concerns expressed by the astronauts were legitimate, particularly those regarding an excess of flammable materials on the command module. However, 25 days before the launch date, there was little motivation to enact extensive changes to the spacecraft's design, and those involved were willing to accept the risk. Unfortunately, the routine simulation on January 27 would offer a cruel reminder that all precautions should be taken. As they made their way to the top of the booster rocket and entered the command module, the three astronauts were confident that the test would go smoothly.

This was because the test revolved around an exercise that was presumed to be very safe. All they had to do was disconnect their module from the launch pad's power and switch it to its own supply. The rocket booster had no fuel, and it was assumed that an explosion could not happen. However, the pressurized module cabin was full of pure oxygen that, under the right conditions, could ignite. Hours into the sluggish test marred by technical difficulties related to communication equipment, a single spark, most likely caused by faulty installations, triggered a fire in the module. As an intense fire erupted, the nylon netting and Velcro, previously identified by the astronauts as dangerously flammable, caught fire and enveloped the astronauts in a terrible inferno.

The fire and toxic smoke likely killed the crew quickly, but the process was slow enough for the engineers to hear the astronauts gradually descend into panic as the fire enveloped them. It took hours for the rescue team to open the module and retrieve the bodies of the crew. In the days following the disaster, Kranz would repentantly acknowledge the many faults in the project and NASA's handling of it. He admitted that the excitement of everyone involved was so great that they routinely ignored problems or unconsciously glossed over them as they hoped for the best. The disastrous scale of such oversights became shockingly apparent only in retrospect once the people on the program could put their biases and dreams aside.

The weight of the tragedy on the conscience of all those involved with the program was probably somewhat alleviated by incredible statements that Gus Grissom had made in the weeks leading up to the launch. Speaking to the press, Grissom asked the public to accept any outcome, including the crew's death. In the minds of the astronauts, there was no room for doubting the importance of the mission. "The conquest of space is worth the risk of life," Grissom explained, adding that whatever happens should not delay the Apollo program.

NASA made the right decision to go only slightly against Grissom's wishes, putting manned flights on hold for over 20 months as crucial issues with the spacecraft were resolved. The lessons learned from the tragedy enabled major safety revisions that greatly improved the command module, balancing the pressurized atmosphere inside the cabin, removing flammable materials, and much more. In total, thousands of changes were made before the famous Apollo 11 made its lunar voyage in July 1969. Although the Apollo 1 trio never got to walk on the Moon, Neil Armstrong and Buzz Aldrin took them there in spirit, leaving a commemorative medallion with their names on the lunar surface.

Recap Questions

- How did each disaster impact public perception and trust in air and space travel?

  _____

  _____

  _____

  _____

- In the aftermath of these tragedies, what safety measures and reforms were implemented?

  _____

  _____

  _____

  _____

- How have these events shaped the importance of ethical decision-making in the realms of aerospace and engineering?

  _____

  _____

  _____

  _____

Chapter 9: Recent Financial Fiascos

The recurring American struggle with economic difficulties has been a strain on the nation's trust in the financial system for centuries at this point. It has been a complex labyrinth of financial downturns, deceitful corporate practices, and mismanagement, juxtaposed with the promise of opportunity and economic freedom that people have come to expect from the United States. This struggle has been a repeating cycle of periodic disasters, usually followed by reforms to curtail the crises.

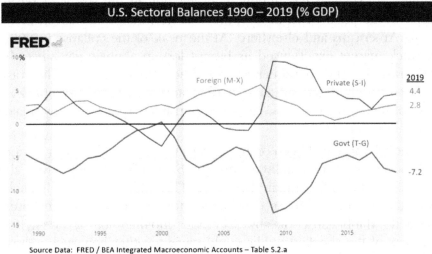

Source Data: FRED / BEA Integrated Macroeconomic Accounts – Table S.2.a

A screenshot of the great recession that took place between 2007-2008.[27]

The ripple effects of these incidents on everyday American citizens have been substantial. Despite hopeful outlooks around the end of the Cold War, such episodes have continued to plague American economic life well into the present day. They also continue to pose a danger to America's stability since the public's trust in the financial systems of the US is an important factor in keeping the economy on track.

The Financial Crisis of 2008

The financial crisis that began in 2007 culminated in the 2008 crash and led to a worldwide crisis known as the Great Recession. On a global scale, the crisis is widely regarded as the worst economic disaster since the Great Depression. It was a calamitous economic episode that's still fresh in memory, with consequences that are being felt to this day. Although the downturn was sparked by the bursting of the infamous housing bubble in the United States, the true, deeper causes of the crisis have been debated at length. The disaster also left an enduring effect on economics and its adjacent discussions, with the popularization of terms such as "too big to fail" in reference to financial institutions critical to the world economy.

The banking system, high-level corporate executives, and, as usual, speculative investors have been frequent targets of criticism regarding the Great Recession. The recession caused a lot of real-world pain across various industries throughout the world, ruining lives and erasing fortunes. As such, it has undoubtedly left one of the strongest recent marks on the public trust in both financial institutions and government, among Americans and elsewhere. At the peak of the collapse in 2007, the stock market experienced its biggest loss in a single day since the 1987 crash, but the consequences would be all but transient. The crash has been widely described as a "perfect storm" of predatory practices, price bubbles, toxic assets, and irresponsible risks taken by major financial institutions.

Although there had been ominous signs for an extended prior period, it all began in earnest halfway through September of 2008 with the sudden collapse of Lehman Brothers. This old, enormous financial institution was one of those considered "too big to fail." As the press swarmed Manhattan's Seventh Avenue looking for answers, few members of the shocked public could piece together how such a crash was possible. Lehman Brothers was a gigantic investment bank with 158 years in the business and an incarnation of the essence of Wall Street.

The federal government also failed to provide concrete answers as to what had happened. The only initial reaction from Washington was that the economy could survive with Lehman, which meant no bailouts for the firm. The US government had already bailed out a number of major financial firms (some of them direct competitors to Lehman) before, so the refusal to rescue Lehman wasn't due to the government's principled stance against corporate bailouts. In fact, it's more likely that government analysts believed Lehman was "too big to fail."

This phrase, certainly one of the most despised that year, continued to echo as things deteriorated. The source of the trouble, as is now widely understood, was in the housing market. The United States has a long history of subsidizing the housing market going back to the 1930s, and the support only grew after World War II. One of the core problems in the immediate lead-up to the 2008 disaster was the unprecedented increase in mortgage debt, which spiked between 2001 and 2007 almost as much as it did throughout all of prior American history.

Coupled with the bubble that roughly doubled home prices in the US, the situation was ripe for trouble. Despite these alarming circumstances, lenders were campaigning aggressively to get as many Americans as they could to borrow more money to buy homes. The campaign went to such an extent that many of the salesmen pushing these mortgages did very little in the way of confirming that the borrowers could actually repay the loans or that they even had assets to cover them. Many of the deals seemed too good to be true, and that's exactly what they were. Sales practices in the 2000s were described as predatory for good reason. All the while, the federal government had little to say.

Lehman was heavily involved in these subprime mortgages, so much so that the firm was under threat of having its credit rating downgraded. The reason why salesmen forewent their due diligence when handing out loans was that the companies they worked for, such as Lehman, had no interest in holding these loans for long. The mortgages would be promptly sold to someone else, and the firms instead focused on increasingly risky investment adventures. There was little concern in the financial world over any of this since the investing community and the banks were accustomed to a stable housing market that they knew had the backing of the government.

Lax government oversight and regulation in the banking sector, which had been on a downward trend ever since the Great Depression, only encouraged risky, irresponsible behavior. The bubble was so tempting that even the oldest, most powerful, and most trusted investment banks couldn't resist. The chickens had to come home to roost eventually, though, and once it all came crashing down, the entire political and financial systems were in a state of utter shock. By the 2000s, the United States economy had become more internationally intertwined than ever, meaning that a collapse of this magnitude would produce unforeseen, devastating reverberations across the planet.

The S&L Crisis

The savings and loan crisis refers to an event in the 1980s and 1990s that wiped out almost a third of America's savings and loan associations. These bankrupted associations, usually shortened to "S&Ls," represented precisely 1,043 or 32% of all such institutions in the US. Saving and loans are both essential aspects of any healthy economy, so the loss of so many S&Ls in a relatively short period was a source of considerable distress in the United States. There were a number of factors driving the bankruptcy of these S&Ls, including growing inflation and a rise in interest rates for banks throughout the late '70s and early '80s.

One immediate problem that these changes caused in the S&L market was that the interest rates on deposits, which were set by the government, became low and unattractive to folks looking to save money in certain institutions. In search of better opportunities, savers withdrew significant amounts of their savings and took them elsewhere, usually to regular banks, inflicting a major blow on many S&Ls. The rise in interest rates also caused long-term, fixed-rate mortgages to lose a lot of their value, which drove down the net worth of S&L associations.

Although S&L associations seem similar to banks on paper, they are not the same. Prior to the crisis, this industry in the US had a tradition of around 150 years, stretching back to 1831 in Pennsylvania. America's S&L institutions, also called thrifts, started out as a rather grassroots initiative by people who wanted to buy homes but couldn't save enough cash. The initiative was an example of communal organizing in the pursuit of home ownership at a time when banks weren't giving out residential mortgages.

To get over this problem, members of S&L associations would pool all of their savings and choose a few members who would be given loans to buy homes. When the money started flowing back in as the borrowing members began repaying their loans, the same opportunity would open up for other members. The system worked well and would grow into a thriving industry over time, although S&Ls, as a rule, remained smaller than typical banks. They were fewer and also commanded smaller assets, but when put together, the 3,000-4,000 S&Ls operating in America by 1980 held around $600 billion in assets, including $480 billion in mortgage loans. In 1980, this was around half of all outstanding home mortgages.

A chart showing the savings and loan crisis.[28]

As the downturn began to spiral out of control, the government first wanted to intervene but then attempted the opposite of intervention. The first legislative response was Jimmy Carter's Depository Institutions Deregulation and Monetary Control Act of 1980. The federal government quickly realized that its regulators were ill-equipped to make any sizeable dent in the massive S&L losses taking place, primarily due to a lack of resources available.

That's why the government then tried to deregulate the S&L industry, hoping that the market forces would run their course and lead to spontaneous growth. Unfortunately, the effect was the opposite of their intention, and the problem got worse, even though substantial growth occurred for a time. As is often the case, the eventual meltdown meant that the American taxpayer would have to carry the weight as Congress saw its way clear to introducing a bailout. By the late 1980s, the industry was subject to extensive reforms and legislation to turn things around.

The initial attempt at deregulation between 1982 and 1985 bore sudden fruits. Since government-imposed interest rates were what choked the S&L industry, an attempt was made to remove various restrictions on the market. Deposit insurance coverage, for instance, was increased to $100,000 from the previous $40,000. This made even the worst-performing S&Ls attractive again for deposits. Different states introduced their own measures, leading to various local excesses. The assets in the industry grew 56%, twice the rate seen among banks.

The new situation allowed for thrifts that would have otherwise gone bankrupt to remain afloat and even experience growth, leading to the emergence of so-called zombie S&Ls. With their newfound liberties, the "zombies" could offer much higher rates to attract more deposits. They then began investing their abundant cash into risky ventures, going for quick yet massive returns. These insolvent thrifts essentially "went for broke," as the brunt of their potential failures would ultimately fall on the taxpayer in the ensuing bailouts.

The failures that started to occur in the late 1980s were rather spectacular, with Texas as a major epicenter. Meanwhile, the underfunded thrifts' insurance fund (FSLIC) was unable to cover the losses of failed investment ventures by irresponsible S&Ls. This led to bizarre incidents such as the 1987 burning of a number of construction projects in Texas, which failed S&Ls had financed as an investment. For the FSLIC, it was cheaper to just destroy the properties than to finish and place them on the market.

By the time Congress passed the 1989 Financial Institutions Reform, Recovery, and Enforcement Act, the disaster had gone beyond all reasonable bounds. Extensive reforms ensued, including the abolition of the FSLIC and the primary thrift regulatory body, the Federal Home Loan Bank Board. It took six years to bring the situation under control by the end of 1995 after the crisis had cost the American taxpayer an estimated $124 billion. Overall, the reform legislation was solid and would provide for more than a decade of stability in the banking sector, which came to an end in 2008.

The Enron Scandal

A few years prior to the 2008 crisis, the United States already went through another major financial scandal involving the Enron Corporation. Enron was an innovative energy company beloved by investors and highly popular on Wall Street. It was also wildly successful, commanding $63.4 billion in assets in late 2001. When it went bankrupt in early December of that year, it was the biggest bankruptcy in American history up to that point. While the 2008 crisis was an enormous process of disaster with endless factors coming together to wreak havoc, Enron's failure was more straightforward, featuring culprits that were easier to identify.

The aftermath of the bankruptcy revealed a tangled web of fraud and financial crimes galore, resulting in lawsuits and prison sentences. Unfortunately for Wall Street, the stench of Enron's financial misdeeds was too strong to escape. The scandal would taint the reputation of the entire stock market and harm its most valuable asset, which is the investment public's trust. The unwritten understanding that financial fraud on an epic scale wasn't a risk for investors looking to buy American stocks was built on that trust.

Enron began with a merger of two natural gas companies under the leadership of Kenneth Lay in 1985 and was named Enron the following year. Enron started out by operating gas pipelines, but once that became less profitable following the government's deregulation of the natural gas market in the early 1990s, Enron shifted focus to trading in energy derivative contracts. In essence, it became an intermediary between consumers and natural gas producers. Jeffrey Skilling was the mastermind behind this new business model. It proved to be a massive success for Enron, turning the company into a household name in relation to natural gas contracts.

Somewhere along the way, however, greed began setting in. Skilling wanted the company to engage in increasingly aggressive trading, which carried more risk. Under his leadership, Enron fostered a culture of intense sales competition, encouraging employees to close as many deals as fast as possible. An employee by the name of Andrew Fastow distinguished himself as the most aggressive salesman, and it wasn't long before he became Enron's CFO.

Such aggressive trading required ways of mitigating the mounting risks, which Enron decided to accomplish through various forms of fraud. The go-to strategy was the use of so-called special purpose entities (SPEs), which helped the company hide billions of dollars in debt incurred from deals and projects that failed. What began as an attempt to lower risk by manipulating the system, using loopholes, and eroding transparency soon became one of American history's biggest instances of corporate fraud. Enron grew at breakneck speed through the 1990s, extending its tentacles into all sorts of markets, even participating in the dot-com bubble.

Enron's SPEs also allowed the company to inflate its profit margins, creating an image of a perfect business model on paper. Investors were hooked, with investments and new deals pouring in from all sides. All the while, Fastow and several executives were scamming the investing public and the company's board of directors. On top of that, Fastow exerted various pressures on auditors from Arthur Andersen, one of the world's five largest audit and accountancy partnerships, to ignore most issues that they inevitably found.

The company made so much money in such a short period that it was guaranteed to arouse suspicions. Various analysts began digging in mid-2001, and it wasn't long until the scandal erupted. The fallout was immediate and all-consuming, leading to the collapse of Enron, which also took Arthur Andersen down with it. A number of executives received serious prison time after the ensuing trials, but the real damage was to America's trust in the financial system.

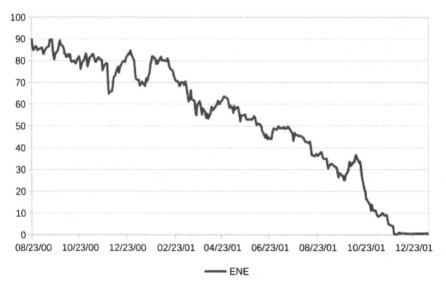

Enron Stock Price from August 23, 2000 to January 11, 2002

— ENE

A chart showing the Enron scandal.[29]

Onlookers realized that even the most promising companies could crash and burn at a moment's notice, which made middle-class investors more reluctant to invest in stocks since they couldn't afford the risk. This consequence is felt to this day, as the number of lower-income Americans participating in the stock market has dropped. Indirectly, this has contributed to the ever-deteriorating wealth inequality in America. The legislative response to the scandal was extensive, exemplified most of all by the Sarbanes-Oxley Act.

The aim of the act, which is still in effect, was to ensure greater accountability for senior corporate executives in regard to the financial statements their companies publish. It's debatable if the bill did much to restore public trust in the stock market. On paper, it does provide for greater and more reliable transparency, but critics have suggested that the bill didn't introduce many measures and government oversights that weren't present before it. According to such criticisms, the bill's greatest effect was to increase the paperwork and bureaucratic processes that public companies have to deal with.

Recap Questions

- How did these financial calamities impact the average American's confidence in economic institutions?

_____

_____

_____

_____

- What were the long-term regulatory and legislative responses to these crises?

_____

_____

_____

_____

- How do these events highlight the interplay between corporate ethics, government oversight, and market dynamics?

_____

_____

_____

_____

Conclusion

Many of the previously discussed historical blunders and their consequences illustrate one important lesson, which is that failures don't have to be final endpoints but opportunities for new beginnings. Lessons learned from these failures have informed important decisions and further progress, and the modern landscape of the United States is the result of these processes. Past missteps have necessitated regulatory reforms, technological development, and cultural shifts that have helped America adapt and overcome challenges. As such, all of these failures of yesteryear have an immense significance that persists to this day.

Some of the failures have been recent, which is why their lessons are still being deciphered and understood. These lessons will also become apparent as long as Americans remember that knowing and understanding history is essential for any society to move forward. Blunders don't make the United States unique in any way. All humans have a propensity to make mistakes, innovate, and eventually evolve. It's the way in which a society tackles its past embarrassments and disasters and the lessons it draws from them that make that society unique. Of course, learning the hard lessons from history and taking them to heart is also important if repetition of such missteps is to be avoided.

For a powerful and influential country such as the United States, perhaps one of the most crucial lessons from the aforementioned blunders is the importance of balance and discussion. With its vast resources and incredible potential, America has the capacity to accomplish incredible feats, but it also has the ability to fail in ways that produce much greater and more disastrous consequences than a lot of smaller countries. Future policies and important decisions must be discussed in a healthy, outspoken climate of understanding and openness.

This is the only way for America to position itself comfortably between isolation and disastrous militarism, government overreach, and uncontrollable markets that speculate their way to collapse – or discrimination and censorship. It's a tough balancing act, but the United States has demonstrated many times that its people have the capacity to walk the fine line and secure a prosperous, peaceful future.

If you enjoyed this book, a review on Amazon would be greatly appreciated because it would mean a lot to hear from you.

To leave a review:

1. Open your camera app.
2. Point your mobile device at the QR code.
3. The review page will appear in your web browser.

Thanks for your support!

Check out another book in the series

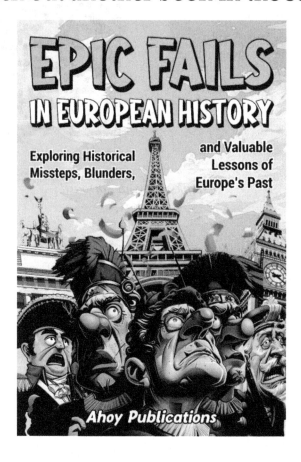

Welcome Aboard, Check Out This Limited-Time Free Bonus!

Ahoy, reader! Welcome to the Ahoy Publications family, and thanks for snagging a copy of this book! Since you've chosen to join us on this journey, we'd like to offer you something special.

Check out the link below for a FREE e-book filled with delightful facts about American History.

But that's not all - you'll also have access to our exclusive email list with even more free e-books and insider knowledge. Well, what are ye waiting for? Click the link below to join and set sail toward exciting adventures in American History.

Access your bonus here

https://ahoypublications.com/

Or, Scan the QR code!

References

Abedin, O. (2016, April 24). Sony Betamax vs VHS: Epic Fails in History #1. Www.linkedin.com.

Bailey, J. D. (n.d.). The Hartford Convention. Bill of Rights Institute.

Bill of Rights Institute. (n.d.). Shays' Rebellion. Bill of Rights Institute.

Case Studies. Business Insider. https://www.businessinsider.com/lessons-from-the-failure-of-the-ford-coke-flopped

Constable, S. (2021, December 2). How the Enron Scandal Changed American Business Forever. Time;

Daugherty, G. (2022, February 14). Why Did the Hindenburg Explode? HISTORY.

Feloni, R. (2015, September 5). 4 Lessons from the Failure of the Ford Edsel, One of Bill Gates' Favorite

forget/2015/03/20/fb525694-ce80-11e4-8c54-ffb5ba6f2f69_story.html

Garner, D. (2010, July 21). Carpet-Bombing Falsehoods About a War That's Little Understood. The New

Grossman, D. (2009). The Hindenburg Disaster. Airships.net.

Harden, B. (2015, March 24). The U.S. war crime North Korea won't forget. Washington Post.

Hayes, A. (2023, June 13). What Ever Happened to the Dotcom Bubble? Investopedia.

hindenburg-disaster-85867521/

HISTORY. History.com. https://www.history.com/topics/19th-century/chinese-exclusion-act-1882

History.com Editors. (2009, November 12). Shays' Rebellion. HISTORY.

History.com Editors. (2009, October 27). Bay of Pigs Invasion. HISTORY; A&E Television Networks.

History.com Editors. (2009a, October 27). Dred Scott Case. HISTORY; A&E Television Networks.

History.com Editors. (2009b, November 9). Trail of tears. History.com; A&E Television Networks.

History.com Editors. (2010, May 10). Stock Market Crash of 1929. HISTORY; A&E Television Networks.

History.com Editors. (2017, August 10). Iran-Contra Affair. HISTORY; A&E Television Networks.

History.com Editors. (2018, August 21). Great Recession. HISTORY; A&E Television Networks.

History.com Editors. (2018, August 21). The Hindenburg Disaster. HISTORY; A&E Television Networks.

History.com Editors. (2018, August 21). U-2 Spy Incident. HISTORY; A&E Television Networks.

History.com Editors. (2018, September 12). Challenger Explosion. HISTORY; A&E Television Networks.

History.com Editors. (2018a, May 4). Rosewood Massacre. HISTORY.

History.com Editors. (2018b, August 21). Watts Riots. HISTORY.

History.com Editors. (2019, August 6). Tulsa Race Massacre. History; A&E Television Networks.

History.com Editors. (2019, February 15). Whiskey Rebellion. HISTORY; A&E Television Networks.

HISTORY.COM staff. (2018, August 24). Chinese Exclusion Act: 1882, Definition & Immigrants

https://billofrightsinstitute.org/essays/shays-rebellion

https://billofrightsinstitute.org/essays/the-hartford-convention

https://history-computer.com/business/the-real-reason-betamax-failed-spectacularly/

https://www.airships.net/hindenburg/disaster/

https://www.history.com/news/2008-financial-crisis-causes

https://www.history.com/news/hindenburg-disaster-zeppelin-crash-why

https://www.history.com/news/remembering-the-apollo-1-tragedy

https://www.history.com/this-day-in-history/the-hindenburg-disaster

https://www.history.com/topics/1960s/watts-riots

https://www.history.com/topics/1980s/challenger-disaster

https://www.history.com/topics/1980s/iran-contra-affair

https://www.history.com/topics/21st-century/recession

https://www.history.com/topics/black-history/dred-scott-case

https://www.history.com/topics/cold-war/bay-of-pigs-invasion

https://www.history.com/topics/cold-war/u2-spy-incident

https://www.history.com/topics/early-20th-century-us/rosewood-massacre

https://www.history.com/topics/early-us/shays-rebellion#attack-on-springfield-arsenal

https://www.history.com/topics/early-us/whiskey-rebellion

https://www.history.com/topics/great-depression/1929-stock-market-crash

https://www.history.com/topics/native-american-history/trail-of-tears

https://www.history.com/topics/roaring-twenties/tulsa-race-massacre

https://www.investopedia.com/terms/d/dotcom-bubble.asp

https://www.investopedia.com/terms/s/sl-crisis.asp

https://www.linkedin.com/pulse/product-failure-history-lesson-1-sony-betamax-vs-jvc-omar-abedin

https://www.vox.com/2015/8/3/9089913/north-korea-us-war-crime

https://www.washingtonpost.com/opinions/the-us-war-crime-north-korea-wont

Kenton, W. (2021, July 30). Savings and Loan Crisis – S&L Crisis Definition. Investopedia.

Klein, C. (2015). The New Coke Flop. HISTORY. https://www.history.com/news/why-coca-cola-new

Klein, C. (2017, January 26). Remembering the Apollo 1 Tragedy. HISTORY.

M. (2015, August 3). Americans have forgotten what we did to North Korea. Vox.

Marticio, D. (2022, January 15). Dotcom Bubble. The Balance. https://www.thebalancemoney.com/what

Rauchway, E. (2018, September 14). The 2008 Crash: What Happened to All That Money? HISTORY.

Robinson, K. (2013, November 22). Savings and Loan Crisis | Federal Reserve History.

Rothman, L. (2014, November 19). What Happened to the Car Industry's Most Famous Flop? Time;

Smithsonian.com. https://www.smithsonianmag.com/science-nature/what-really-sparked-the

Stromberg, J. (2012, May 10). What Really Sparked the Hindenburg Disaster? Smithsonian;

Time. https://time.com/3586398/ford-edsel-history/

Time. https://time.com/6125253/enron-scandal-changed-american-business-forever/

Whitten, D. O. (2019). The Depression of 1893. Eh.net. https://eh.net/encyclopedia/the-depression-of

Williams, N. (2022, July 28). The Real Reason Betamax Failed Spectacularly. History-Computer.

Www.federalreservehistory.org. https://www.federalreservehistory.org/essays/savings-and-loan-crisis

York Times. https://www.nytimes.com/2010/07/22/books/22book.html

Image Sources

[1] https://commons.wikimedia.org/wiki/File:Signing_of_the_Declaration_of_Independence_4K.jpg

[2] https://commons.wikimedia.org/wiki/File:James_Bowdoin_II.jpg

[3] https://commons.wikimedia.org/wiki/File:Alexander_Hamilton_by_John_Trumbull,_1806.png

[4] https://commons.wikimedia.org/wiki/File:James_Madison(cropped)(c).jpg

[5] https://commons.wikimedia.org/wiki/File:Jim_Crow_sign,_anti-Latinx.jpg

[6] https://commons.wikimedia.org/wiki/File:Dred_Scott_photograph_(circa_1857).jpg

[7] https://commons.wikimedia.org/wiki/File:The_Chinese_Must_Go_-_Mayor_Weisbach_poster.jpg

[8] https://commons.wikimedia.org/wiki/File:ChineseExclusionSkeletonCartoon.jpg

[9] bec, CC BY-SA 4.0 <https://creativecommons.org/licenses/by-sa/4.0>, via Wikimedia Commons. https://commons.wikimedia.org/wiki/File:Unemployed_men_during_the_Great_Depression.jpg

[10] https://commons.wikimedia.org/wiki/File:Hazen_S._Pingree_Cyclopedia.png

[11] Made by ed g2s • talk., CC BY-SA 3.0 <http://creativecommons.org/licenses/by-sa/3.0/>, via Wikimedia Commons. https://commons.wikimedia.org/wiki/File:NASDAQ_IXIC_-_dot-com_bubble_small.png

[12] Mosedschurte, CC BY-SA 3.0 <http://creativecommons.org/licenses/by-sa/3.0/>, via Wikimedia Commons. https://commons.wikimedia.org/wiki/File:Cold_War_WorldMap_1962.png

[13] https://commons.wikimedia.org/wiki/File:John_F_Kennedy.jpg

[14] https://commons.wikimedia.org/wiki/File:Saddam_Hussein_in_1998.png

[15] Júlio Reis, CC BY-SA 3.0 <https://creativecommons.org/licenses/by-sa/3.0/>, via Wikimedia Commons. https://commons.wikimedia.org/wiki/File:US_map_1864_Civil_War_divisions.svg

[16] https://commons.wikimedia.org/wiki/File:Ku_Klux_Klan_Virginia_1922_Parade.jpg

[17] https://commons.wikimedia.org/wiki/File:Wattsriots-burningbuildings-loc.jpg

[18] https://commons.wikimedia.org/wiki/File:US_64th_regiment_celebrate_the_Armistice.jpg

[19] https://commons.wikimedia.org/wiki/File:Korean_War,_train_attack.jpg

[20] https://commons.wikimedia.org/wiki/File:USAF_F-16A_F-15C_F-15E_Desert_Storm_edit2.jpg

[21] https://commons.wikimedia.org/wiki/File:15-09-26-RalfR-WLC-0098_-_Coca-Cola_glass_bottle_(Germany).jpg

[22] Michael Barera, CC BY-SA 4.0 <https://creativecommons.org/licenses/by-sa/4.0>, via Wikimedia Commons.
https://commons.wikimedia.org/wiki/File:Vintage_Grill_%26_Car_Museum_May_2017_16_(1958_Edsel_Skyliner).jpg

[23] Maximus saldana webb, CC0, via Wikimedia Commons.
https://commons.wikimedia.org/wiki/File:Betamax_Logo_1975.webp

[24] https://commons.wikimedia.org/wiki/File:Wright_First_Flight_1903Dec17_(full_restore_115)_(cropped).jpg

[25] https://commons.wikimedia.org/wiki/File:Hindenburg_disaster,_1937.jpg

[26] https://commons.wikimedia.org/wiki/File:Apollo_1_crew.jpg

[27] User: Farcaster, CC BY-SA 3.0 <https://creativecommons.org/licenses/by-sa/3.0>, via Wikimedia Commons.
https://commons.wikimedia.org/wiki/File:Sectoral_Financial_Balances_in_U.S._Economy.png

[28] https://commons.wikimedia.org/wiki/File:Mortgages_and_interest_rates.webp

[29] Nehrams2020 (original), User:0xF8E8 (SVG), CC BY-SA 3.0
<https://creativecommons.org/licenses/by-sa/3.0>, via Wikimedia Commons.
https://commons.wikimedia.org/wiki/File:EnronStockPriceAugust2000toJanuary2001.svg

Made in the USA
Middletown, DE
13 December 2024

66713970R00070